Fiona Horne has been a practising Witch for fourteen years. She is also a journalist, singer, solo music artist and radio and television presenter.

Fiona lives in Melbourne with her snake familiars, Lulu and Sebastian. *Life's a Witch!* is her third book.

Also by Fiona Horne

Witch – A Personal Journey
Witch – A Magickal Year

Random House Australia Pty Ltd
20 Alfred Street, Milsons Point, NSW 2061
http://www.randomhouse.com.au

Sydney   New York   Toronto
London   Auckland   Johannesburg

First published by Random House Australia 2000

National Library of Australia
Cataloguing-in-Publication Entry

Horne, Fiona, 1966– .
Life's a witch! : a handbook for teen witches

ISBN 1 74051 022 4.

1. Witchcraft – Australia. 2. Incantations. 3. Magic. I.
Title. II. Title : Handbook for teen witches

291.330994

Cover photograph by Monty Coles
Cover styled by Mark Waziak/The Look
Cover hair and make-up by Marie-Louise Cannon
Design by Gayna Murphy/Greendot Design
Illustrations by Sergio Medina/Every Picture Tells a Story
Typeset in 12/15 pt Bembo by Midland Typesetters
Printed and bound by Griffin Press, Netley, South Australia

10 9 8 7 6 5 4 3 2

Life's a Witch!

A Handbook for Teen Witches

Fiona Horne

RANDOM HOUSE AUSTRALIA

Thanks!

A huge thanks to Aaron Mostert, Annabel Cooney, Ashlee Chapman, Jackie Davie, Simon Graser and Stephanie Bendixsen for appearing on the cover with me! Also thanks to Gwendolynne, Fox 14, Third Millennium, Versace, DKNY, Bettina Liano, Brave, Wayne Cooper, Saba, Peter Lang and Charlie Brown for their generous support and supply of clothes for the cover photo.

Enormous thanks to Michael and Sue Gudinski and David Smith for their generosity and friendship. Once again, thanks to my dear buddy, Liam Cyfrin, who has supplied his indispensible advice, wisdom and insight so generously! Blessed Be! Thanks also to Jessica of the Nightstar Teen Pagan Network who agreed to be interviewed for this book.

Big thanks, too, to my best mates Krista and Tanja for supporting me through the hectic time of writing this book – I love you! Lots of love also to my management team: Terry, Melissa, Justin, Rochelle and Alli; and to the Random House team, especially Roberta, Jane and Benython.

This book was written at 'Penrith', Mount Macedon.

Contents

Introduction

Teen Witches and would-be Witches seem to be every-where these days. They meet after school or find time alone to do spells to help them pass tests, to attract boyfriends or girlfriends, or to help them get along with their parents. And at night, when other teens are out getting drunk or stoned and switching off from life, Teen Witches are out under the starry sky, turning on to the magick of life.

Some are the children of those who got into the Craft back in the '80s when the Wiccan population of the world skyrocketed. Others come from more conventional fami-lies and have been inspired to explore Witchcraft by movies like *Practical Magic* and *The Craft* or TV shows like *Charmed*. A majority of them are girls but Hollywood often misses the mark by a long shot in depicting Witchcraft as a girls-only club, and more and more guys are finding that they have an important place to fill in the Craft too.

The great thing about Teen Witchcraft is that it's

empowering and positive, encourages confidence and boosts self-esteem. Teen Witchcraft strengthens an individual's respect and relationship with the Earth, friends and family.

Some adults, including some older Witches, get very hung up on teens practising Witchcraft and put it all down to them following a temporary fashion. There's probably a little truth in that for some teenagers – after all, some of the most strait-laced adults around today used to be hippies in the sixties or punks in the seventies! But for many of today's teens, their fascination with the Craft isn't going to be 'just a phase' but the beginning of a lifelong adventure.

Your teenage years are an ideal time to begin the study of Witchcraft. Young minds are loaded with passion and wonder about the world – channelled well, these energies are perfect for the experience of magick.

One theory of the derivation of the words 'Witch' and 'Wicca' is that they come from an old Anglo-Saxon word 'wicce', meaning wise, which raises the issue: 'Can a teen be wise?' Looking back at *my* teen years, I am sometimes horrified at the risks I took and the dangerous situations I put myself in, but somehow escaped from (more on that later!). But if I had been practising Witchcraft I know for a fact that I wouldn't have found myself in those situations in the first place. You can't practise the Craft without picking up at least some of its wisdom, and so, most Teen Witches are in a much stronger position that I was at their age. This is because Teen Witches respect the sacredness not only of all life, but particularly their own. They know that their lives, bodies, thoughts – the totality of their being – is sacred and powerful. They don't need to prove anything to anyone. Teen Witches trust their intuition and work to develop it and their personal power to be the best that they can be.

All these are things older Witches also need to work on – in fact, developing a deeper understanding of your-self and developing your personal power are never-ending experiences along the magickal path of a Witch's life.

There are many, many books about Witchcraft available now, but not a lot for Teen Witches. One of the reasons for this is that, up until recently, the attitude was pretty much that teens were too young to handle the responsibility of guiding themselves along their own spiritual path. People thought that the energies which can be conjured up during ritual and spell-working are too much for teens to handle.

However, the reality is that teens can pick up any book about Witchcraft and start trying it, and this is where there can be some problems. I think the biggest problem is that you may find the books too much to absorb, and the ideas not specifically geared to the things going on in your own life. The other problem, of course, is the temptation to try certain forms of magick without having first learnt their dangers. The classic example would be to try a hexing spell you find in a book somewhere, without having assimilated the knowledge that while hexing people sounds power-ful, it's actually very disempowering and brings more trouble than it's worth. Discovering this too late can cause all sorts of problems to develop in your life because you're dabbling in the 'dark side' of magick without sufficient knowledge and experience.

Another traditional danger to the inexperienced occultist (more often than not, a non-Witch) is experi-mentation with Ouija boards and the like, which, when approached carelessly is about as smart as getting into a car

with an absolute stranger. There *are* dangers (although magickal catastrophes happen far less than those who fear the Craft like to believe) but it's in the nature of teens to want to experiment with life. It's not really much different from sex. Apart from a few extremists, no-one suggests that it is something you should never do under any circumstances, and experienced people know the potential physical and emotional dangers involved – hence them wanting to protect younger people from stumbling into these dangers through inexperience. However, it's no good just saying 'Don't do it' and leaving it at that. Some teens avoid the dangers by following that principle but others are going to experiment no matter what they're told. The best thing adults can do is offer the knowledge teens need to stay safe and happy.

In my opinion the bottom line is that, when treated responsibly and respectfully, Witchcraft is great for teenagers. If you're lucky enough to be in a Witchy family, it's an ideal way to share and communicate with your relations. And if not, you're discovering your spirituality and power for yourself, which can strengthen you in so many other aspects of life as well. I know that every teen who writes into my website says they feel better about themselves as a Teen Witch. They feel they have a unique identity and are special, loved and at home in the Universe.

WELL, FIONA, WHY WEREN'T YOU A TEEN WITCH?

Beats me! No, seriously, I had a very magickal vibe early in my life which saw me communing with nature spirits in my bushland home, casting spells with my intuition as my only guide, and tapping into some innate inherited Witchy wisdom (my blood is German/Hungarian after all!). I also played mad Witchy games with my girlfriends, and one of my favourite memories is when my best friend Linda and a few of our friends were at a sleepover.

We were all tucked away in Linda's bedroom with the lights out, and one girl was lying on the floor with the rest of us kneeled around her – one at her head, one at her feet and two either side at her waist. We each placed just our two index fingers under her and then Linda instructed us to repeat what she said and did. In grim unison, we chanted 'She is dead, let her rise from her coffin'. To our astonishment, as we raised our arms, rise she did, as light as a feather until she was stretched out on the total of eight fingers, well over our heads. My distinct memory is of a choking presence so that my eventual gasp of surprise got stuck in my throat and came out as a loud gurgle, at which sound we promptly dropped her.

It was the most surreal experience I'd ever had at that young point in my life, though at the time I didn't equate it with anything magickal. I didn't pursue any other kind of magickal processes until I was about twelve and feeling very isolated and disillusioned. To rebel against my Catholic upbringing I began to explore Satanic ideas and started lighting black candles while saying the Lord's Prayer backwards and reading scary horror novels. In retrospect, that phase was totally silly and really didn't have anything to do with my later discovery of real Witchcraft. It was just one of the ditsy things you do to prove you're independent from their parents. I found my little foray into Satanism disempowering, and actually quite boring. Its emphasis on fear and oppression reminded me too much of what I didn't like in my Christian religious education. (As far as Satanic stuff goes I explore the subject in detail and point out how different it is from real Witchcraft in my first book, *Witch – A Personal Journey*.)

From the age of fourteen I pretty much lost the plot completely and got wrapped up in peer pressure, boys, trouble and started to forge for myself a very difficult and ultimately confusing and heartbreaking path. I say 'forged for myself' because I did have a choice, but I didn't have enough respect and love for myself to see that the choices I was making were only making things harder, not easier.

Right at the end of my teens, I was drawn to Witchcraft and entered society's acknowledged age of adult life, although I'd lived the life of a self-supporting adult from the age of fifteen – living out of a home with a job. However, it wasn't until I was eighteen, and dealing with life after a particularly dark period, that I really discovered my inner magick and a sense of wonder and excitement woke up inside me. Over the next several years, I went through lots of ups and downs but never lost my sense of self again, and whenever things were hard I knew I had the tools to work through it and learn. For a long time I lived by the edict 'The more sorrow carved out of you, the more joy you can contain.' I started to understand the cyclical nature of life and stopped feeling the overwhelming sense of futility and angst that had shadowed so much of my early years. Having said that, I still experienced lots of self-doubt, but I knew that eventually the dust would settle and I would see the glowing green 'Exit' sign and move on to happier times.

Your teen years are possibly the most challenging of any but they are the gateway to the rest of your life: what you make of them will form the foundation of how you launch yourself into the future. But try not to feel pressured by it – your bodies are going through natural hormonal changes that would freak out an over-committed body builder on illegal steroids! Every fibre of your being is waking up but at the same time wanting to run away from the awakening pressure of the outside adult world. When I was a teenager I felt so old, so wise, so worldly – but at the age of thirty-four, I look back and see that really I was *so young*, and not taking the time to enjoy it!

There's a gorgeous song called 'Don't worry – be happy'. I think if Teen Witches had an anthem this would be it. One thing I've learnt as my life has got longer is that you don't need to sweat the small stuff – especially when you're a Witch. The Universe always has something bigger around the corner.

TIPS ON GETTING THE MOST OUT OF THIS BOOK

This book is just the beginning. In it you will find rituals and spells that are written just for you as a teenager finding your way in the Craft. Some things will be easier to understand than treatments of the same subjects in other books written for an older perspective. Some things will be harder because they will be encouraging you, as a Teen Witch, to dig deep inside and learn about all the magick that is inside of you.

Use Your Intuition: At times you won't be able to follow everything to the letter and this is when you need to stop, listen to and trust your gut instinct. A lot of the spells and guidelines in this book are quite in depth and demanding. This is because I am confident that Teen Witches have a greater ability to grasp magickal concepts and work with magickal energies at this time of human evolution than some would give them credit for. At the same time I have included lots of quick-fix, instant spells that will work quickly and reliably when fuelled with an honest heart and honest intent. The more demanding spells are just as achievable as the 'easy' ones and often ultimately more rewarding because the more effort you put in and the more focused you are, the better the results will be.

Don't worry! You can't do anything absolutely, irrevocably and horribly wrong (as long as you don't break the Witches' laws). You'll almost certainly make a lot of small mistakes – but that's good and they will help you learn. But if you get an inspiration to do something, maybe a particular spell or ritual, and it resonates beautifully and strongly within you (and again doesn't break any Witches' laws) then go ahead and try it!

Research and Learn: Use this book as a map to lead you further along the path – all the answers aren't

THE WITCHES' LAWS

1. Do what you want to do as long as you don't hurt anyone.
2. Do what you want to do as long as you don't interfere with another's free will.
3. That which you send out returns upon you, threefold – minimum!

A note on the third law: It's not quite as simple as 'I'll do nice things so three times as nice things will come back to me' or 'I won't do bad things because I don't want three times as bad things to happen to me' though you'd have to admit it makes a better case for blessings than cursings! The third (or threefold) law exists to keep Witches responsible and aware of the ramifications of all their acts. Real Witches don't seek to harm others, however bad the individual's behaviour might be, because the act of healing wrongdoers, or binding them, to prevent them doing further harmful things, is far more powerful and effective, and it won't bounce back on the Witch. They also don't do things to achieve a selfish goal. As mentioned in my earlier books, most Witches discover that they work better magick for a friend than they do for themselves, so once again, on a purely practical level, selfish magick really loses out. Real Witches are aware that everything is interconnected and value balance well ahead of short-term personal gain.

here, but a lot of the questions that you need to ask are. Again this book is a starting point to hopefully encourage you to continue exploring the wonderful world of the Craft. Use the suggested reading and the websites at the back to take you further and give you a deeper insight.

If you find a word or description of something

you don't understand, just flip to the glossary ('Gobbledy Gook!') at the back of the book where I have put together a list of explanations for unusual terms. If at any point you are reading a spell you want to try and you don't understand why something is being done, or what the Goddess or God mentioned represents – research it straight away (you can start with the chapter 'Magickal Meanings' at the back of this book) and make some notes in your magickal journal or Book of Shadows.

By the way, my book *Witch – A Magickal Year* has comprehensive lists of the magickal qualities of herbs, planets, numbers – anything that you can't find in this book is listed there. In this book I have also tried to keep the majority of herbs, crystals and other objects suggested down to a choice of easily accessible and obtainable items.

Something to Remember: There is so much Witchy information around it may seem bewildering – so many Goddesses and Gods, herbs, crystals, spells, paths and traditions to understand and remember. If you identify yourself strongly as a Teen Witch, the Craft is likely to be something you will explore for the rest of your life. So take your time: allow your personal magickal world to weave itself within and around you. It will ebb and flow in varying intensity over the years so don't feel that you need to know everything at once and don't be afraid to make mistakes. As long as the Craft is meaningful to you, and as long as you feel magickal, then you are on the Path. Enjoy the journey!

In Your Own Words

While preparing for this book, I invited Teen Witches to write in to my website with any queries they might like to have published and answered. Here's a selection of some interesting ones.

```
i have attended circle with my
mother and enjoyed it. i am also
interested in jesus and the bible.
how does it all seem relative as
the teachings are so different - or
are they?

love amelia
```

As I wrote in my first book *Witch – A Personal Journey*, I dig Jesus! I went on to say that 'if he was around today, with his values of tolerance, acceptance, respect for Nature and fellow people, he'd be a Witch!'

One of the main differences between the Craft (and many other spiritual paths) and mainstream forms of Christianity is how we see the nature of religion. I think mainstream churches seem to look at religion as if it were science, a system with theories that are either right or wrong: if their religion is right, anyone else's must be wrong. The Witch sees religion as being more like culture or language. If an Aboriginal dancer moves completely differently from a classical ballerina, we don't say that the Aboriginal person is dancing wrongly. If a French person calls her house 'ma maison', we don't say that she's using the wrong words. And similarly, if a Buddhist seeks spiritual union through one method or philosophy, a Jew another way, and a Moslem another, we don't claim that one is doing it the right way and the others are messing it all up (or that all three are barking up the wrong trees and only Witches are going about it the right way).

Witches feel that when you're wrong it's important to learn about lots of spiritual traditions and let yourself be drawn to the one best for you. The best for me was Witchcraft since it makes the most sense to me personally. Read the Bible if you're drawn to it and see what you think. I found it contradictory, disempowering, confusing and depressing – but you might find otherwise! A lot of very good people do. Remember as you read it that really it's a collection of works written over a long time and edited and translated over and over again, and that to really come to terms with the book is the study of a lifetime, not something you'd gain from a single reading of a particular version. There's been oceans of blood spilt over the centuries through people believing that they were experts on the subject when they're really only beginners.

I have to say that I don't relate to Jesus as he's described in the Bible as well as I do to his presentation in alternative writings about him, like the book *Jesus the Man* by Barbara Thiering.

```
krystal
age 15
what about nightmares? i mean
i would love to read about
nightmares, i get them all the time
and i would like to know what other
witches get them as well

blessed be
shahla (my name)
```

I'm sure lots of Witches get nightmares – I certainly do. They are generally a symbol of growth and change within the individual where your subconscious is shaking off the past or dealing with present hang-ups by releasing them as dreams. Unless your sleep's being seriously disrupted by nightmares, it's best to let them run their course rather than trying to use spells to suppress them. The emotions they release will only have to find another outlet if you block the dreams. Oh, and contrary to what our TV Witch equivalents experience so often, our nightmares are very rarely prophetic or indications that we've slipped off into some strange demonic world!

```
Dear Fiona,
You totally rule girl. I have got
both your books and they are so
good. all the extra things you put
in them with all the interviews and
experiences are truly great.
```

I never thought of doing
witchcraft until I read your first
book *Witch - A Personal Journey* off
a friend who had bought it and I
thought it was sooooo cool. Then I
went and bought your second book
and it totally rocked as well.
So I would really appreciate it if
u could put this letter in your
book so when I buy it and see it in
there all my friends will be
jealous and it would be really cool
because you totally rock. Thanks
heaps!

Daisy

Well, OK, strictly speaking Daisy isn't asking a question, but who can resist that sort of flattery?

I'm glad you liked the books so much, Daisy, and that they helped you along your path to the Craft. I should say, though, that it's not really my intention to encourage people to take up Witchcraft exactly since we Witches don't go in for trying to convert anyone. But I guess a lot of Witches would say that one particular book or magazine article motivated them to begin their magickal studies so I'll take it as a compliment that mine did the trick for you!

Dear Fiona,
I had two Jehovahs Witnesses arrive
on my doorstep today and were
talking to me about the bible & my
belief in God, etc. Upon saying I
was practising witchcraft, they took
off in a flash. What is it about

witchcraft that sets them on edge?
(Considering witchcraft is not
satanic)

Danyon

For the main part it's because there is still, after all this time, the misconception that Witches worship Satan. I have tried to make it clear in all three of my books that, since Satan is a Christian concept, the guy is most definitely not a part of Witchcraft at all! After all, who needs a nasty character like that in their mythology? Not the Craft, that's for sure.

Some fundamentalist followers of other religions seem to get some sort of peculiar excitement from the notion that there are evil Witches in the world, but I can't see the attraction myself. Surely there are enough real problems to face in this world without inventing imaginary ones?

You've discovered a great trick for getting rid of them though, if you don't want them in your space. I'll definitely say the same next time they knock uninvited on my door!

Fiona,
If possible, in your new book could
you include a self initiation spell
for some of us who are solitary
witches? Also a list of how to meet
others of like mind would be
helpful in your new book, as I find
it is pretty difficult to meet
others who are also interested in
the craft.
    Those who are high priestesses and
high priests - are they required to
have followed the path and studied

it for a particular amount of time,
and who decides whether they may
become a high priestess/priest?

Thanks Catherine-Silverdragon

Check out the self-dedication ritual on page 37 and you
might like to try the initiation experience offered as part
of my Wikid Witch Kit (stockists are listed in the Suppliers
list at the back of the book). The unique website that is a
part of this kit is a great way to link up with other Witches
too. The message board on my website www.fiona-
horne.com always has heaps of Witches on it and also, you
can check out the suggested websites at the back of the
book for more contacts.

As far as High Priestesses/Priests go, the thing to bear
in mind here is that, along with thousands of very indi-
vidualistic, mainly solitary Witches (like me!), there are
also lots of Wiccan traditions, clans and tribes out there.
Among these there's a whole range of different styles of
working magic, different titles and degrees and different
initiatory requirements. You can read up on some exam-
ples of these in various books and websites, but if you ever
choose to join a formal group (usually called a Coven or
a Grove), you'll still need to learn that group's particular
system.

Usually a High Priestess or High Priest (or HPS and HP
for short) is part of a Coven and it is their Coven that
bestows this acknowledgement. They (often a female and
male partnership) may be the permanent principal organ-
isers of the group, although in other groups, the positions
are temporary, being titles given to the Witches who are
running a particular ritual, rather than running the whole

Coven. In this case, the positions will be given to different qualified people at different times to avoid the group becoming too hierarchical.

Solitaries are not generally considered High Priest/esses, though they may hold that rank if they were once part of a Coven. I am not an initiated High Priestess though I have the knowledge and experience that would qualify me as one if I were part of a Coven. Several Witch friends of various traditions have told me that they'd happily grant me an honorary HPS status at some of their Circles on the basis that they consider I know my stuff well enough to do the job, even though I'm not of their tradition. This sort of professional courtesy is quite common among Witches and shared workings happen much the same way as a marriage between a Jew and Christian might be jointly officiated by both a Rabbi and a Priest or Minister.

It is not the ultimate goal or seal of approval for a Witch to be called High Priest/ess. The ultimate goal is to never stop learning and evolving as an adept Witch.

```
fiona,
i have been practising witchcraft
for around 3 years now and your
books are some of the best i have
read. I am now only 15 and still
interested in wicca and similar
subjects as i have been brought up
with a witchy history thanks to my
grandmother and met many interesting
people (including you!). i was
wondering if you had any tips on
what sort of things should be
practised every day and on
heightening psychic energies. i am
```

grateful for any ideas you might
have. thanks heaps and good luck
with the new book it'll be great
i'm sure!

Blessed Be
love Catherine

I suggest good and visualisation exercises like the ones in
'Hot Spell Tips' (see page 71) which will help focus and
intensify your psychic powers. In addition to doing these
daily, the best tip I can give is trust that you are psychic
and that it is an innate human ability, available to anyone
who chooses to uncover it.

There's such a thing as Witch blood, though, and you
might've been lucky enough to score some through your
Grandma. If not, don't panic – hard work can generally do
just as much as a little magickal sparkle in your family's
genes.

Hi Fiona!
My name's Dorota, and I'm 17. I've
read both of your books and I think
they're great. Your way of
expressing your passion for wicca
and all things related is fantastic
and it's really easy to relate to.
I've been sort of practising wicca
for a couple years now, and one
thing that keeps on cropping up and
still kind of confuses me is that
it's so hard to practise something
which is so pro-life and pro-
mysticism, while a lot of people
these ·days seem to be wanting to

```
reduce human contact and seem to
have less respect for human life.
How do you cope?

Thanx. Blessed be.
```

I know what you mean! As a nature-worshipping Witch it can be very confronting when you realise the extent of ecological and social strife this planet is in. You can only live your life the best way you can in acting locally as you think globally. Do healing spells for the planet and get active in environmental support and action groups. Use your net-surfing time to help the plight of the world's hungry by visiting www.thehungersite.com and doing a small something for the planet's rainforests at www.therain-forestsite.com. Shop, consume and dispose in an environmentally aware way and do at least three nice things for people out of the blue every day. As the bumper sticker says – 'Practise random acts of kindness and senseless beauty'.

Don't feel swamped by the problems in the world – more than ever teens are shouldering the burden of mistakes that previous generations have made. The sense of responsibility can be even heavier for a Teen Witch. Once you've started getting positive responses to your spells, you can easily feel that it's up to you to get the whole planet back on track. I don't want to discourage you from doing your bit but there's just so much one little Witch can do to help a planet largely run by shortsighted cynics, so keep trying but don't try to carry the whole weight of the world on your back. I often think of the Chinese proverb, 'The journey of 1000 miles begins with the first step' – just take that first step and keep going!

Dear Fiona,
This is a question I would be
interested to see you answer in
your new book. I have bought both
your previous books and I found
them very interesting and
enlightening. I know many Teen
Witches have the same problem as
me. I'm 14 and I have been studying
and practising Wicca for 2 years
now. I have tried a few spells
(sometimes with friends) and did a
lot of meditation exercises and
recently started celebrating the
Sabbats. Even though I do all this,
I still feel like there is
something missing in Wicca for me.
My motivation and enthusiasm is
unpredictable and erratic. I was
wondering if you have ideas or
suggestions for me to keep up the
practising and regulate it? I feel
that this is truly my religious
path but it gets hard to sit down
and do something seriously while I
am swamped with my schoolwork and
social life. Sometimes it seems as
though I am missing the point on
Wicca completely. Can you please
help me?
Thank you very much! =)

Blessed Be,
Helena*

As Witches, the one thing we need to be constantly aware
of is the flowing of the tides of life and seasons. Some of

our inner seasons will align themselves to those in the natural world outside but there are also subtler tides and rhythms in our energies that we need to be conscious of. So, as I mention in my introduction, the way in which you express your Craft will ebb and flow in varying intensity throughout your life as you explore the path created by others and go on to forge your own. Don't feel you have to celebrate every Esbat or even every Sabbat in a full-on elaborate way. With my schedule sometimes the best I can manage is a quick Witchy prayer on a full moon, and the last time I went to a Sabbat festival was over a year ago! I always recognise and celebrate the Sabbats, but sometimes it might just mean lighting a candle and meditating for a little while on the meaning of the event. All through this book there are quick, easy little things you can do to keep you on the Path even if it seems that you're only moving a millimetre at a time for a little while.

Why not do some spells to help you cope with your schoolwork and social life, and don't be afraid to take your time with your magick – you've got your whole life ahead of you!

```
Hi Fiona!
I really loved your first 2 books,
keep up the good work!
  My question is about astral
projection. Have you tried it and
does it work? Is it harmful at all?
Thank you. :o)

Bright Blessings
Hayley (16)
```

I used to actively practise astral projection when I was in my early twenties. I had more time then and would meditate for hours, trying different techniques to master and control it. The strangest experience I had was when I was following instructions from a book which said I should sit and meditate, then focus my mind's eye on seeing myself sitting opposite me. I managed to do this quite clearly, and then my other self got up and went out the window! Then my consciousness shifted into that self and I was standing at the edge of the ocean (which was just down my street). It was night and I jumped in and swam underwater. I felt the liquid as a cold pressure around me, but not how I would normally feel wet. Then I banged my head really hard on something which made me wake up back in my body. I felt a bit sick and the top of my head hurt.

The next day I walked down the end of my street and looked out to sea. There was a big tanker moored not far offshore waiting for permission to enter Sydney Harbour. Was that what I banged my head on?

If I astral travel now I tend to do it spontaneously and it usually happens when I have insomnia (which is caused by stress). All of a sudden I'll feel nausea and then I'll be looking towards my feet but they seem at least ten metres away, and everything goes into tunnel vision – but my eyes are shut. It's at this point I could go off wandering but the intensity of the event usually yanks me awake. It isn't harmful and can be experienced in varying intensities depending on how prone to it you are or adept you become at it. It's not an essential part of Witchcraft, and it doesn't happen like you see it on *Charmed* when a demon spirit can be walking around in the physical world giving the girls a hard time!

Some Witches find that they can be almost too loosely connected to their physical bodies at times, and a common cause of excess weight gain among Witches occurs when they turn to food as a way to feel more grounded and integrated with their bodies. If you ever experience this 'astral looseness', give up on any conscious attempts at projection for a while and concentrate on grounding instead – but preferably not through a week-long binge at McDonald's!

```
Dear Fiona,
I and a few friends have been
interested in Wicca for the last
six years. I would just like to
know how long it takes before you
can call yourself a witch?

Tara,16
```

That's a trickier question to answer than it might sound. In the more formal traditions of the Craft, the title of Witch is one you gain at your initiation. For solitary followers of the Craft, it's really something you need to feel for yourself. Of course, since the Craft is so flexible there's nothing to stop someone calling themselves a Witch after performing one spell or reading a single book on the subject. Whether that sort of 'Instant Witch' would be acknowledged as such by other, more conscientious Witches is another matter though. In general, while people in the same tradition use another person's knowledge of that group's magick as a guide to whether they're genuinely a Witch, most people in the Craft just seem to go on a gut feeling. There's just a particular energy that we recognise in each other.

As to where this energy comes from, well, some are born Witches, some are made Witches and some have Witchiness thrust upon them! Most of us who've been in the Craft a good while have met people who are just absolute natural Witches, although they mightn't be initiated, well-read on the Craft or even aware of the fact themselves. And we've met one or two people who've gone through all the right training, reading, exercises and initiations and just don't seem to have the spark at all.

If you know other, long-term Witches you can probably tell if they have the spark and whether it's something you can recognise in yourself as well. If not, well, clearly the first person you'll have to examine for the spark is yourself. Beyond that, I think when you have a clear understanding that a Witch works to honour, protect and heal nature, recognises the Goddess and God (or Lady and Lord) as symbols of the Divine, lives by the three laws of Witchcraft, and seeks to expand their knowledge of the Craft by reading books and casting spells, then you'd be pretty safe in considering yourself a Witch! Whether you've been doing this for six years or six weeks the most important thing is your recognition of the magick you contain within you.

When you are ready you could consider a self-dedication rite (see page 37) and then, in time, a self-initiation, but you have to be absolutely committed before attempting them, leaving perhaps a minimum of a year and a day between dedication and initiation. Also see the chapter 'What is a Real Witch?'

```
Fiona,
I'm a 17 year old female from
brisbane who lives in a sharehouse
with four other people. I sometimes
```

find it difficult to do rituals and
other witchy stuff because the
others ask questions. I've tried to
explain to them (the two housemates
who don't understand) why i need to
be left alone at these times but
they just don't get it - they
interrupt me all the time! I find
it hard trying to fit rituals into
the timeslots in which those two
aren't home but it's really hard.
   I don't have enough room in my
room to do rituals and stuff and I
can't go to parks etc around here
either because the council hire
security guards to keep 'weirdos'
out. any suggestions?

Gwen

Witchcraft is about being resourceful and understanding that, more often than not, it's not the big showy rituals and spell castings that give you the most magickal feeling and the deepest sense of what it is to be a Witch, it's the little things. The stillness in the air just before the sun rises as you light a candle in honour of its growing presence is magickal. Burning beautiful incense and meditating on sending love to those who need it as you hold a crystal and stare at a candle flame is magickal. These are small, easy, unobtrusive things you can do. You don't need to be calling out to the Goddess and waving your athame around all the time!

When I was on tour with Def FX (my old band) I had to share a room with one of the boys. At these times my mobile altar was a crystal, a feather, a tea light candle (rarely

lit), a glass of water, and a beautiful Goddess card drawn
by Elizabeth Kyle, a wonderfully talented and magickally
inspired New Zealand artist. I would just set this up on
the night-stand next to my bed and throw it all back in
my bag the next day as we moved on to another town. I
would do my Witchy ritual work as I sang on stage, conjuring up energy as well as channelling it and sending it
around as a healing and empowering force.

Use your intuition and find new ways to go about things
rather than giving up and doing nothing at all. When you
can, practise the formal disciplines, but take the pressure
off yourself and do a 'Keep out of my space spell' to keep
your friends out of your hair!

Until then, a really good exercise (one I recommend all
Witches to learn how to do) is to visualise in complete
detail every step of yourself performing a full Circle-
casting, getting all the gestures and words perfect.
Developing this skill will repay the effort time and time
again in life when you need to perform a Circle but can't
do the whole thing physically.

```
Hi Fiona*,
I'm a HUGE fan of yours! I just
wanted to take this opportunity to
say that you are a true inspiration
to me. When I was diagnosed with
cancer in November 1998 you helped
me get through so much with your
books. Through your introduction to
Witchcraft I was able to find
spiritual fulfilment in a time when
I was experiencing a great lack of
faith and reasons for living and I
am eternally grateful for that. I
```

have a few questions that I would
love for you to answer for me:
 1. I know that when casting circle
it is important to cut a gateway if
you are going to leave the circle
during the ritual but what if
animals are in the room? My dog is
with me most of the time and I
don't like her being kept out of my
room. What can I do about this,
especially if she wanders in and
out?
 2. My brother has asked me to be
his sponsor at his Confirmation (he
attends a local Catholic school
where it is compulsory). This is not
important to him and he has always
been interested in Wicca since
seeing my books around. I have told
him that he is too young to make
any decisions about his faith yet
(he is 12) but I would like to
possibly tie in some Wiccan
practices on his Confirmation day
either before or after the mass. I
know that may sound strange but I
have heard of Christian Wiccans and
wondered if you had any ideas?
 Well, thanks again and sorry about
the long email. Fiona - keep on
doing what you do because you make
a lot of people happy and never
forget that.

****Blessed Be****
Cara (a. k. a. Magickal_princess)
Age: 17

Blessed Be★ Cara!

As far as your dog wandering in and out, it can weaken a Circle a little; and if he's not your familiar and finds magickal energies conjured in Circle a little intense, it's not surprising he needs to leave. Maybe you could try the spell that is suggested in the familiars chapter in *Witch – A Magickal Year* to see if you can gently attune him to your magickal work. An animal wandering in and out creates less of a problem than a human so don't worry about it too much, but if you feel your Circle is 'seeping' energy then use your gut instinct to go to where the 'leak' is and seal it by channelling blue light from your athame or power finger.

About your brother's confirmation – I was confirmed, so it doesn't have to affect his interest in Witchcraft and, yes, there are some Christians open to the practices of Witches (and, though being a Christian Wiccan sounds like quite a juggling act, certain Witches do, for instance, invoke the energies of Jesus and Mary into their Circles, along with other manifestations of male and female divine power). Perhaps at the end of the day you could both do a little dedication to the Goddess. In being confirmed he is being presented to the aspect of Christian deity, the Holy Spirit of God, so you could balance it by honouring the Witches' female deity by lighting a silver candle and reciting the Charge of the Goddess together (hopefully under a full moon, if by some lucky chance his confirmation is on the same day!). Have him make an offering to the Goddess – perhaps cut a little of his hair and bury it under a flowering plant (jasmine, gardenia or white rose would be great), take a sip of some juice (preferably apple) and then pour a little on the ground as he says 'Great

Goddess, I give thanks for the bounty and beauty of my life.'

> Dear Fiona,
> How do you usually tell if someone
> is your soul mate? What are the
> signs? Do you know much about this
> kind of thing ...?
>
> Love and Light,
> Carla Raelene xxoo

It's funny, I used to be so hung up on finding my soul mate — and now it's the last thing on my mind! When I did spend a lot of time thinking about finding mine, I used to go to my favourite tarot reader and ask her if my current boyfriend or the guy I liked was my soul mate. Sorry, if I sound flippant! But I'm definitely making fun of me here, not you.

As to the signs ... well, you might just have a strong gut instinct when you look into their eyes. However, I have found over the years that even the closest friends drift away sometimes. Ultimately I think every human has lots of soul mates, lots of people to bond with, share energy with, learn from and love.

> Fiona,
> i heard that if you do a spell that
> someone else has done then you
> share their karma. is this true?
>
> Kate

Nah ... an old wives' tale methinks!

Dear Fiona,

My name is Cassandra, I'm 11 years old and I have recently become interested in Witchcraft, particularly spells, the tools of Witchcraft, and their unique properties. Here are some questions I thought might be good to include in your new book.

Is Wicca and Witchcraft the same thing?

Could you tell me something about Pagan and Satanic practices and how they differ from Witchcraft?

Where are the best places for performing spells and rituals? And do you need to open and close a circle when doing spells?

How does one find a coven to join? And what should you look for when doing so (ie: should I be careful)?

Thank you for taking the time to read my questions. I hope they will be useful for your book.

Yours sincerely,
Cassandra

Wicca is a path of Witchcraft, like Catholicism is a path of Christianity. There are many different paths of Witchcraft: for example, Hermetic, Gardnerian, Alexandrian and Dianic to name a few. They are all part of the same whole, just different ways of viewing, exploring and contributing to it.

All Witches are Pagan, meaning they are part of a nature-worshipping or Polytheistic religion. However, not all Pagans are Witches. Satanic practices are a knee-jerk reaction to Christianity and are not based on real Witchcraft.

The best places for performing spells or rituals are out in nature, but any space can be cleansed and consecrated to work in – that's what a Circle casting ritual does. As I say in the chapter 'Circle Casting and the Tools of Witchcraft' there are different methods for casting Circle and I have also suggested a couple of less complicated options for Teen Witches. Not every spell and ritual requires you cast Circle, though it's often preferable as it helps to intensify energies and make workings more effective.

There are a few ways you can find a coven, all of which I mention throughout the rest of this book. I recommend chatting to other teens on my website, or better still, contacting the Nightstar Teen Pagan Network (the address is in the chapter 'Twinkle, Twinkle, Little Star').

```
Dear Fiona!!
U're definitely my fav witch :) i
have just discovered the Craft for
half a year, and only own 2 books,
which are yours! You have given me
so much inspiration and insight. I
just want to say thank you so much!
  i also have a query that i've
been wondering about for a while. i
am Chinese and immigrated here a
few years ago. i have been
wondering if it would be OK to
write Chinese in my BOS or use
Chinese in invocations, etc. i've
been doing it, but not so sure
```

```
about if it's appropriate to do
that.

Love you, and thanx 4 ur time :)
Rain
```

It's absolutely fine! Your Book of Shadows (BOS) is your personal record of your magickal work and journey as a Witch. However you want to express yourself in it is up to you.

While much of Wicca is heavily influenced by ancient Celtic, Nordic and classical religious beliefs, the Craft is a truly multicultural spiritual path and is enriched by the culture of every person drawn to its ways. In recent decades, the Craft has been blessed with teachings from Aboriginal, Native American, Slavic and African cultures to name just a few, and there are so many Wiccans now from Jewish stock that they coined the word 'Jewitch' to describe themselves!

Personally I would love to hear Wiccan invocations and chants in Chinese!

```
Dear Fiona,
I have a question for your book:
Sometimes when I was just beginning
(and even now, when I've been pagan
for years) I started to believe
that you're just making it all up,
that magick didn't exist and the
Lady and Lord weren't within me.
When I start to doubt like that, it
sometimes takes me a really long
time before I feel the magickal
charge again. Did you ever doubt
```

yourself and your path like that,
and if you did, how do you handle
it?

KaOdorite, 17
(means Dancer of the Fire in
Japanese)

By the way – thank you for this
book on behalf of everyone who is
going through now what I did when
I was younger and trying to find my
path while everyone told me that
I wasn't old enough to believe in
anything. I'll still appreciate it
because I haven't completely grown
out of my indecision and doubt.

I often fell in and out of the Craft when I first started, especially if something went really bad. This was before I had
fully comprehended the cyclical nature of living, and the
light and dark aspects of the Path. I thought Witchcraft was
like a big band-aid that would cover up all the hard stuff
and give me easy answers – but the best thing about it is
that it's not!

Even now I don't walk around feeling the Lady and
Lord within me – however, I sense the polarity and com-
pleteness of the Divine and that all humans, female and
male (in fact, all creation), are a part of that. When my
magickal charge is low, I take some time out and bond
with nature (check out the chapter 'It's Only Natural').

You are young and you're going to find the Craft will
get easier and harder in ways you can't anticipate in the
coming years. Hang in there, and don't be rigid with your

beliefs and expectations. Allow them to shift and evolve and reflect your growth as a human and Witch.

```
Fiona,
I would like to ask your advice in
how to handle a problem as you may
have come across something similar
before. My long time boyfriend is a
Christian and believes that pagans
worship the devil and he really
hates it when I look at anything in
a shop which has something to do
with Witchcraft. How can I make him
feel better about Witchcraft?

Kristen
```

Give him this book to read! Or perhaps better yet, my first, *Witch – A Personal Journey*, in which I interview real Satanists and show how they have nothing to do with Witchcraft. As I have said many a time to my parents the first time they hassled me about my Craft, 'You have more to do with Satan than I do, you're Christian. I don't believe in Satan. He's a part of your religion not mine!'

If you wanted to spend the time you could tell him that Paganism is an older religion than Christianity and a lot of the Pagan Gods and Goddesses, as well as Pagan holy days and festivals, were absorbed into the Christian tradition and just given different names.

You might also remind him that more people than ever have suffered and died in the name of the Christian God than in the name of the Witch's Goddess, and that even the Pope himself recently felt compelled to apologise for the abominations of the Witch hunts of the Dark Ages.

But perhaps instead of simply trying to out-argue him, you'd do better to point out that Witches strongly adhere to the notion that there's enough room in the world for everyone's beliefs and you'll let him get on with his if he lets you get on with yours. Really, the only aspect of certain forms of Christianity that Witches take exception to is their contempt for the deeply-held beliefs of others.

Not that all Christians advocate narrow-mindedness though. Many do take the words of their gentle, compassionate founder to heart and there's a new type of Christian who not only tolerates but welcomes Witches in the world. There's an article written by one on my website www.fionahorne.com. Maybe your boyfriend could read that.

In the end, the best (though by no means the easiest!) way to deal with ignorance and prejudice is with knowledge and love.

What is a Real Witch?

Even though you've just read the Teen Witch question chapter, I have picked out two particular emails that were sent to me because they address some of the most common questions asked by Teen Witches.

Hiya Fiona,
Just an idea for the book. A question too I guess. Watching films such as *The Craft* and TV shows such as *Sabrina*, *Charmed* and *Buffy*, magick is glorified so easily. It comes up as being the answer to all of life's problems and looks absolutely brilliant. I guess in a way it is. Not strictly speaking though. These shows have some of the ideas and 'morals' of witchcraft correct, but many things they promote just don't happen in true

magick. I see these shows as promoting witchcraft as the answer to anything and everything and also helping teens to think they are witches when they really aren't.

These days it is all too easy for teenagers to open a magazine, find a 'spell', do it and call themselves witches. They have no idea what magick really is though. They don't know where it really comes from or what it really means. Do you have any advice for true teen witches on how to stand apart from all the rest? This may sound a little crazy as all of the true teen witches I know don't boast about it and generally don't tell anyone. It's just very hard to be accepted as a true witch, especially by older, more experienced witches when there are so many 'try hards' running around today. Maybe you could write a little section on the true meaning of being a witch. You could explain that just because you do a spell from a magazine, own a witchcraft book or buy a Spellbox set and do what the instructions say, that that doesn't make you a witch. I think it is important and needs to be said in a book such as yours that is being aimed and promoted towards teenagers.

Thanks
Jackie (age 17)

Jackie raises an important point – it does seem that anyone can, for example, buy a copy of (the wonderful) *Witchcraft* magazine, try a spell and say they are a Witch. But this doesn't need to put a Teen Witch's nose out of joint! If there are kids at your school who you think are Witch-wannabees and going around banging their chests for attention and threatening to cast (not very nice) spells on all and sundry, just ignore them. Don't give them any of your energy. There's room in the universe for everyone, so just go about your own business. However, if someone is really driving you nuts carrying on that they are a Witch and it seems like a lot of hot air, just start talking to them about the Craft or offer to do some basic ritual work with them – this will quickly sort out whether they're pretenders or they know what they're talking about!

HEXING – YOU'RE BEING PARANOID

Some Teen Witches write to tell me they are worried about someone casting a bad spell on them. Let me assure you that ninety-nine per cent of hexes work only if you are susceptible to them. Nearly all cultures have traditions of hexing or cursing, and most of these practices work on a single principle: the spell isn't what does the work. It's the victim's belief that he or she is just that – a victim – that gives them trouble. So, step one in keeping hex-free is to remember you're not a victim.

You can open yourself up to certain energies, and by the same token if you don't allow things to attack you they won't. You can diffuse negativity – it's like blowing smoke away or pouring water on a fire. If you feel like you've got a lot of negativity around you and you want to clear the air try the following spell.

BLOW IT AWAY SPELL

You will need:
* Salt
* Four sticks of incense (rosemary, sandalwood or Nag Champa are good – or any blend for banishing), or four charcoal blocks in dishes of sand with incense sprinkled on top
* A glass of water

Sprinkle the salt around you in a deosil (anticlockwise/ sunwise) direction. Stand a stick of incense at the north, south, east and west quarters. Light them, and as they burn, take some time to focus on who you think has hexed you or the situation you feel negatively trapped in. Then go to the first stick of incense (with the water) and say:

Smoke within this space,
Capture the trap that's placed.
One, two, three,
I blow away its hold on me.

Gently blow the incense smoke so that it leaves the salt circle. Then put out the incense in the glass of water (pour water on the discs). Now do this to each incense quarter.

When you have finished, push the Circle of salt open in a widdershins direction (clockwise against the sun in the southern hemisphere) as you say:

I release any sadness bound to me,
For the good of all,
So Mote It Be.

Remember! Doing any hexing yourself is *not* recommended. Real Witches know that to really get in touch with their abilities they need to respect the existence of hexing but also be aware that it actually weakens and ultimately destroys a Witch's power. I have discussed hexing at length in *Witch –*

A *Personal Journey* and *Witch – A Magickal Year* but I think quoting one of the Witches' laws is appropriate here for Teen Witches – 'As you send out so returns threefold' . . . if you're lucky! It may hit a whole lot harder than that.

This is why it's very unlikely that you or anyone you know will ever encounter a real curse. Those who know their Craft are too smart to use them; and those who might consider a hex are generally total newbies without the skills or experience to control the spell.

My friend and long-time Witch, Liam Cyfrin, shares his wisdom here:

In many respects, the word 'Witch' has more in common with terms like 'artist' or 'magician' than 'Buddhist' or 'Hindu'. While various types of self-dedications and initiation are commonly used in the Craft, they are better understood as being primarily rituals of recognition than as admissions to a club. One 'becomes' a Witch gradually through attempting to be one, just as artists or musicians earn the right to their titles.

Of course, anyone who can hold a paint brush can claim to be an artist and anyone who knows how to bang out two chords on a guitar can profess to be a musician. But whether they – or anyone else – truly believes these claims is another matter. We judge musicians by their performances and artists by their art, and we can generally sense when we're in the presence of talent, regardless of whether the precise form of the artistry is our cup of tea. The same thing precisely applies to Witchcraft.

Real Witches stand out by moving far beyond the dabbling, try-a-spell-or-two stage and going the long haul, and not bragging about what they do. (See page 35 for the Four Magickal Principles, especially 'To Know' and 'To Be Silent'.) Sure, you can be initially attracted to Witchcraft's exotic and rebellious face, and now, more than ever, Witchcraft is being packaged commercially as a form of entertainment instead of a genuine spiritual path as more and more spell-kits, articles and magazines pop up everywhere. But real Witches get past that dabbling stage pretty quickly and find that the glamour and mystique are still there but in a more subtle and profoundly empowering way that goes far beyond shock value and trendy fashion appeal.

Real Witches worship nature and always work to recognise and connect with the cycles of the seasons and see them reflected in all facets of our lives. We honour the concept of the Goddess and God (or Lady and Lord) and we recognise that this divinity exists within us as well as without and has many faces and forms. We work magick by harnessing the elemental forces of nature – air, earth, fire and water – and focus and direct these energies with our will, and further fuel them with our emotions. We seek to help and heal rather than harm and destroy, though we understand that a full life is not only about the good and easy times but also the difficult and dangerous.

As for older Witches not taking Teen Witches seriously – well, ignore 'em! Every Witch is an individual and some are more intolerant and crabby than others: no-one is perfect! Some Witches out there seem to have forgotten that they were new to the Craft themselves once and had to learn as they went. Some of them also seem to have very little sympathy or respect for any young would-be Witch following a different path from the one they took themselves. Strangely enough, though, many of the same people are big on the notion that a Witch shouldn't have any authority higher than his or her own conscience and intuition.

On the bright side though, there are plenty of older Witches who, when they consider their own first steps, are very supportive of the new Witchy wave and are happy to admit that they're envious of the resources around for today's new Witches. So be assured there are plenty of older Witches you can learn from and be inspired by, and who won't be so quick to judge you. If you are genuine and on the Path, they will sense this in your presence and hear it in your words. If a potential teacher or older Witchy person rejects you when you know you're genuinely a seeker, then you don't want their approval anyway. I meet *heaps* of Teen Witches and wannabees in my travels and, believe me, I can tell the difference! Which is to say, I don't shun the wannabees, I just try to give them some constructive advice.

```
Dear Fiona,
I'm having a bit of trouble. I'd
like to be a witch, and I consider
myself a witch. But it's just that
the books I've read say that I must
search for the Lady, and that I
must be initiated. I'm a lone
witch, though wouldn't mind finding
a coven. It's just that I'm keeping
this a secret. I can't keep an
altar because my parents don't know
```

and I don't want to tell them. I
was wondering, what does it take to
be a witch, and can you be one even
though you aren't initiated?

  Also, I wear a necklace with a
pentacle, it has a little tear drop
hanging off it. Is it still a
pentacle, and is it wrong for me to
wear it when I'm not a 'real'
witch?

Rainbow Love (age 14)

As far as having to hide your Witchy interests from your
parents, I address this at length in the chapter 'Doing What
You Will'. Right here, though, I can say if you are scared
they won't understand your interest, it's probably because
you fear them judging you as silly or perhaps even thinking that it's something to do with evil and Satanism.
Unfortunately this is a fairly ingrained misconception
about Witchcraft that is thankfully shifting, so why not try
sharing a bit of information about what Witchcraft really
is with them? Perhaps give them a look at this book. Really,
there's so much literature around now debunking any connection between the Craft and Satanism that you can't help
feeling that the only people still believing otherwise are
those who passionately *want* to believe it!

Real Witchcraft isn't about wearing a pentacle (though
heaps of Witches do, either as jewellery, often beautifully
styled and embellished, on clothing, or as tattoos). However,
it is about taking the first steps and if this means buying a
spell kit and trying it or reading a book and identifying
with the word, 'Witch', then that's OK.

As far as needing to be initiated into a Coven to be considered a real Witch – well, like thousands of Witches the world over, I have never been initiated into a Coven. I have been a Solitary for fourteen years, though I certainly have had a lot of contact with other Witches in the last few years! People project energy and real Witches, as solitary as so many of us are, are eventually drawn together, and many Witches find group rituals very rewarding and appropriate for the way they choose to experience their Craft. But that doesn't mean you have to be part of a Coven.

On page 37 there is a 'Self-dedication ritual' which you can do to formally declare to the Universe that you are a budding Witch. Further along the Witchy path of your life, you will have other opportunities to make formal declarations of your Path and Craft and you may end up being initiated into a Coven or other particular Wiccan tradition. You are a real Witch as long as you are genuine and honest. Some Witches are obviously more adept than others but every super-together and powerful Witch had to start somewhere!

The final word on 'Am I a Real Witch?' is this – don't worry, be happy and just do it.

TEEN COVENS

A Teen Coven does not have the hierarchical structure like some adult Witch Covens. The adult Coven structure reflects the levels of knowledge and experience of individuals within the group.

A Teen Coven is more like a working group of equally experienced people exploring their Craft together. You can celebrate Sabbats and Esbats, do spells together and share your problems and successes. I know a group which regularly organises trips to interesting magickal places and group shop-athons for Witchy clothes and tools. Another has a garden plot at a communal garden and grows magickal herbs there.

A Teen Coven can be a fantastic support group as you inspire and help each other to keep going with your Craft and use it to make the most out of life. There should be no leader in the bossy sense of the word – everyone should share tasks and knowledge. Having said that, if everyone is happy for one person to organise and co-ordinate things that's fine too. It's important to remember that everyone is equal, and that ego trips are for idiots, not Witches.

THE FOUR MAGICKAL PRINCIPLES – To Know, To Dare, To Will, To Be Silent

The principles speak for themselves really, but I'll spell them out for you in more detail!

To Know: Witches are seekers of knowledge. We know we can never stop learning, about ourselves, others, the world, magick, life – everything! We are also strong in our identity as Witches and trust and believe in our methods.

To Dare: Witches do not live life with blinkers on: we face the onslaught of existence, good and bad, head on and take full responsibility for our actions. We are not afraid to make mistakes in our quest for knowledge and personal development, and we do not shy away from the 'dark side' – not in the sense of valuing evil but in accepting that pain, loss, hardship

and death are all necessary and unavoidable parts of
life. We confront and explore our fears and
subconscious, and we embrace the light and dark of
life, all shades of grey and all the dazzling colours in
between.

To Will: Witches work magick by focusing our will.
The cornerstone of our spell-casting is our will, and
understanding the precept that magick is 'The Art of
Changing Consciousness at Will'. In other words, the
world will answer according to the questions you ask
of it. Witches understand that they can change their
life, that they have a say in it and that they can use
their will to work to assist others.

To Be Silent: Perhaps because for so long Witches
were persecuted – and even now we still cop a lot
of flak – 'to be silent' can be seen as a protective
statement. But it also means that we don't need
approval, gratuitous attention and we don't proselytise
(attempt to preach and convert). We also know that
to talk (let alone brag) about our magickal
undertakings will dilute their potency. So when spells
are in progress we don't talk about them (that would
be like digging up a seed you just planted to see how
it's going).

    As I am a very public Witch, the To Be Silent
edict is an interesting one for me. I have a few basic
ways I relate to and practise it. For a start, in social
situations I never announce that I am a Witch.
However, if someone asks me if I am I will answer
honestly. I see one of my roles as a Witch as a
provider of information for those who choose to
read, listen to and perhaps absorb it in some way.

Even though I have now written three books and appeared on countless TV and radio shows, done public rituals and written songs about the Craft, there is still a part of my practice that I keep just between me and the Universe. Witchcraft is an occult tradition and always will be – there will always be a hidden element which is fuelled by every individual Witch. We come into this life alone and we go out alone, and it's in our deepest, deepest sense of self that the roots of our individual Craft anchor.

WHITE WITCH? BLACK WITCH?

Often when I am on television or a radio show I will be called a 'White Witch'. I always correct them gently by saying, 'No, just a Witch'. To call myself a White Witch is reinforcing the stereotype that some Witches are inherently bad and evil. Life is never white or black, only both and all shades of colour in between.

Witchcraft is about the totality of life, all experiences, good, bad and indifferent. Witchcraft is not a light-weight, New Age philosophy that runs away from darkness and danger or seeks to convert everything into 'white light': it's gutsy and potent, honouring the balance of creation and destruction.

SELF-DEDICATION RITUAL

The following ritual is something you can do to formally announce to the Universe that you are a budding Witch. It's not a substitute for the years of knowledge and practice that you need to accumulate to become an adept Witch, but it will align your energies with that of other like-minded souls. As a Teen Witch it will give you a sense of credibility and focus as you embark on the Path. Before you do this, though, you should read the next chapter 'Circle Casting and Tools' (as well as the rest of the book!), which explains all the things you need to know and understand about doing rituals and spell work.

Best time: A full moon
You will need:
* Three oak leaves
* A piece of white cord that is exactly your height
* A white candle
* A black candle
* A lock of your hair
* Three drops of your blood
* A sharp pin (to prick your thumb with!)
* A medium sized cloth bag, preferably decorated with a pentagram
* A garland of ivy woven with seasonal white flowers (whatever is blooming at the time)
* A special garment never worn before (if you choose not to be skyclad)
* Special anointing oil. Mix the below ingredients together to form a paste:
    ☾ Ten mls of almond oil
    ☾ One teaspoon of sandalwood powder, mixed with half a teaspoon of crushed sea salt
    ☾ Three drops of lavender oil

The Ritual: You first need to gather the oak leaves from a living tree. The oak is one of the most sacred and powerful trees and it is a direct link to the Celtic origins of Wicca. Its presence denotes wisdom, which is what you are seeking as a Witch.

Kneel at the base of the tree and ask its permission
for three leaves:

Oak tree, I ask thee
For your leaves of three,
Your blessing bestow on me,
Oh mighty oak tree.

If three leaves flutter down, fantastic! Gratefully accept
these, otherwise carefully pluck three from a single branch,
bow three times in thanks and then walk away without
turning your back for at least twenty paces.

Place all your objects on your altar and prepare yourself
for the ritual by bathing. If you can jump in a freshwater
lake or the ocean, great! Otherwise, have a bath with a cup
of strained rosemary tea added, or perhaps a bath bomb
(the salt is purifying). Either stay skyclad or dress in your
special garment, and place the ivy and flower garland on
your head.

Cast Circle with the full ritual, using frankincense as
your incense. Anoint yourself with the paste at your third
eye and heart, and the tops of your feet as you say:

Lord and Lady, bless me
As I undertake a journey
With no beginning and no ending.

Sit and meditate for a moment on how you feel about
being a Witch – the things you hope to learn and achieve,
both physical and mystical.

Now light the white and black candles from the same
flame as you say:

As above, so below,
Light and dark,
So my journey goes.
My heart is true,

My intention pure,
The Craft of the Wise
I seek to pursue.

Meditate on the candle flames and contemplate the fact
that being a Witch involves challenge and risk. You will be
called upon by the Universe to prove your worthiness of
the title. Absolutely every Witch I know has had to confront some of life's toughest issues – it seems to come with
the territory – but every challenge makes us stronger,
better, more accomplished. In walking the path of Witchcraft, you are not hiding away from the realities of life, but
facing them head on – good and bad.

Hold the oak leaves in your hands and say:

The wisdom of those gone before
I seek to honour,
The wisdom of those to come
I seek to inspire.

Put a drop of your blood on each of the leaves and place
them back on the altar. Now take up the cord that is the
measure of your height. Raising it in offering, say:

Lady and Lord, accept this measure
Of my commitment to Witchcraft.
I present myself to all Creation
And ask to be acknowledged as Witch.

Now cut a lock of your hair and place it, the cord and the
leaves into the bag; then close Circle.

This bag needs to be kept somewhere safe where it will
not be disturbed. You may like to repeat this ritual further
down the track and embellish it at your own discretion as
your experience and knowledge grow. Each time you do
it, take a new measure of your height and, instead of the
oak leaves, you may choose another natural object that

represents qualities you are seeking to develop as you grow as a Witch.

Note: The anointing paste that you created can be used again in private rituals to help focus your psychic abilities. Just apply some to your third eye before casting Circle.

JUST A THOUGHT

Remember that when it comes to Witchcraft we work on Goddess time – that is, time can not only be experienced as a straight line of past/present/future (linear) but also as 'round', with all things happening at all times. So don't worry that you're casting a Witch's Circle and practising magick before you've even formally declared you are a budding Witch. If you are drawn to the Craft to the point of making the self-dedication above, then the ability to do the ritual is within you. Just trust and work with your intuition and desire.

HEREDITARY WITCHCRAFT

I am adopted and it was quite a revelation to find out at the age of twenty-seven that I was half Hungarian and German. On my father's side I'm Jewish (though of course I can't inherit this as it is a matrilineal culture, but I have the genetic memory of my ancestors), and on my mother's side I'm Lutheran.

I have sometimes wondered why I have such a strong calling to Witchcraft but on finding out my ancestry I stopped questioning why Witchcraft would resonate through every fibre of my being. I choose to believe that my Celtic/Teutonic bloodline is related to my attraction to the Craft, but more and more people without a drop of the stuff are being drawn into Wicca these days, just as lots of European people have found their spiritual home in, say, Asian, African and Jewish spirituality.

Wicca, currently the most accessible Path of Witchcraft and one that I focus my travels upon, originated from ancient Celtic culture and methods of worship.

History notes that the Celtic people originated in an area that is now France and southern Germany. Their culture spread extensively and included central Europe, Britain and Ireland, before they were conquered by the Romans by the first millennium BCE.

Celtic culture was so sophisticated, and had such a wonderful spiritual and artistic heritage, that it's not surprising so many people are relating to and reviving it today. (On a lighter note, for example, the practice of 'touching wood' to ensure luck and good fortune comes from the Celtic and Druidic practice of honouring trees as sacred, magickal and the cornerstone of life.) By the way, I want to make clear that Wicca is not a genuine revival of traditional, pre-Christian Celtic religion but simply draws some elements and a lot of inspiration from it.

I also found out recently that the last Witch to be burnt at the stake was Janet Horne in 1722 in Scotland, and my adopted family tree can be traced back to Scotland. This, combined with my European heritage, makes me feel I can certainly claim an inherited interest in the Craft. Not that this is essential though – let's remember that we are in a way related to every single human being on the planet, because we are all part of the same biosphere of planet Earth. So we can feel proud of, and connected to, any calling that resounds within us.

BURNING TIMES

This is a very sad time: from approximately the beginning of the 14th to the end of the 18th centuries, the 16th being the worst, the Church, already well experienced in the persecution of so-called heretics, extended its hostility to those alleged to be involved in Witchcraft.

It's sometimes said that millions were tortured and killed after Witchcraft charges, but although there can be no precise numbers, historians now believe this figure to be far too high. Even so, the most conservative historians seem willing to allow that anything from 40,000 to 60,000 women, men and children were murdered for supposedly practising Witchcraft, while others believe the death toll might have reached 100,000. At the height of this persecution, there were hardly any village healers or midwives or independent religious leaders – all having been killed for genuine or imagined Witchcraft. In reality, the people killed were anyone who threatened the powers of the Church, and individuals whom people of power had a grudge against. (If you want to understand how hysteria and ignorance can fuel this kind of hatred and insanity, hire the film of the Arthur Miller play, *The Crucible*.) Witchcraft is no longer an offence punishable by death, though it is still illegal to tell fortunes in Tasmania!

GAIA

(Pronounced 'guy-ah.') I relate very strongly to the concept of our planet as a self-regulating, living organism – Gaia or Mother Earth. Nothing is separate; each component affects and interrelates with each other. The waterways are her blood; the air, her breath; the mountains, her children; the fire, her heart. As organisms we evolved specifically from the stuff of this biosphere – so we are not separate from this earth, but totally bonded with it.

Witches know that our greatest responsibility is to tread as lightly as we can on this planet, to heal the damage done and prevent future damage as much as possible. Recycling, reusing plastic bags and containers, composting vegetable matter and minimising your waste, and being an active supporter of conservation groups (check out the environmental group links at www.fionahorne.com) are all practical ways to practise 'Gaia consciousness'.

Witches can also work magickally to honour and heal Mother Earth. This simple ritual can be done either alone or with other Teen Witches.

Gather together in a park or on a beach. Stand, holding hands, and feel the earth beneath your feet and the sky above your heads. Breathe deeply and feel yourself centre and ground. Become very aware of where you are in the Universe, standing on the surface of a planet that floats in infinite space. Think about the myriad of different life forms that share this planet with you. When you are ready say individually:

Gaia (our/my) Mother Earth,
(We/I) offer you my respect and love;
Thank you for your beauty and bounty;
As Witch and human with you (we are/I am) one.

Now do something to honour where you are – it may be picking up all the rubbish you can see and putting it in recycling bins, it may be planting a tree. It may be just sitting, looking and pondering in wonder at how absolutely amazing the natural world is.

Circle Casting and the Tools of Witchcraft

TO CAST A COOL CIRCLE

Here's all you will need:

* Incense or a feather
* Candle (new and lit, or unlit if you can't light flame in your room)
* A bowl of salt, sand or soil, or a favourite crystal
* A bowl of spring water (or tap water if that's all you can get)
* Athame or wand (or just use your power finger)
* A bell or gong (not essential as you can clap your hands instead)
* A plate with some food (perhaps biscuits you have made or something yummy you have bought) and a chalice or glass of juice – or whatever you prefer
* A table or surface to place all these things on!

One of the most daunting things for me when I started practising Witchcraft was casting Circle. There seemed to be so much to remember and I was forever getting confused about which colour candle was required in which Quarter and which Guardian was which. I was worried I'd do something wrong and my Circle would not protect me from negative energies, or that I'd do something out of order and the Circle wouldn't exist at all. The information I read in various books would just blur, my mind would switch off and most of the time I wouldn't end up doing anything at all.

What I am hoping is that this chapter will help you get your head around the basics of Circle casting so you can really get started with working magick. If you want to try a more elaborate Circle casting, check out my first two books or any of the plethora of other books on Witchcraft.

Note: All the directions I give below are for people living in the southern hemisphere – if you read something different in another book, it's likely to have been written for people living in the northern hemisphere.

There are lots of different methods and approaches to casting Circle and just about all of them will work if (a) they make sense to you, and (b) you follow the same pattern in as many of your workings as possible. There's no single, correct and only way to cast Circle – your task is to discover the one best for you personally. The most important thing to understand and ensure is that the procedure that you choose is the one that resonates most strongly within you. You are creating a sacred space in which to work magick, and that's the most vital thing for you to remember. Understand that it's how intensely *you* feel the space to be special and sacred that will determine whether your Circle *really* exists or not.

Having said that, there's no merit in trying to invent some brand new system for yourself. By adopting one of the standard forms, you're making it easier to share your Circles with other Witches if you choose to, as well as linking into a well-established pattern within the collective unconsciousness.

Your Circle is just that: a circle, with four quarter points aligned to the four cardinal directions of the compass (North, South, East and West), each one attributed to one of the four elements of traditional Western magick (Fire, Earth, Air and Water). You need to invoke the four elements into your Circle so that the magick you create in the spiritual or astral realm has a way of manifesting in the physical realm. I used to think I would never get my head around the directions, the quarters and all the correspondences, but it can be done! So here it is, short and sweet.

THE FOUR ELEMENTS

There are four elements: Air, Earth, Fire and Water. Each 'lives' in a different direction:

Air – East (because that's where the sun rises and is the place of new beginnings, which is something Air is good at blowing into your life). Air is represented by incense (or a feather if you can't light incense sticks and the like at home).

Earth – South (because it's as far away from the equator and the light and heat of the sun as you can get, and Earth is about dark, contemplative energy). Earth is represented by salt, soil, sand or a crystal.

Water – West (the sun sets there and it is a place of
completion where all things come to rest. Water
represents all the emotions, and how we feel about
things is what dictates what we ultimately end up
doing). Water is represented by a bowl of spring water
(or tap water if that's all you have).

Fire – North (the direction of the equator and the
intense presence of sun's fiery heat). Fire is
represented by a candle (or, if you can't have fire at
home, something that is red or orange – you could
paint a burnt stick with red paint, for example, or
have a new red unlit candle).

GUARDIANS OF THE QUARTERS – Our Magickal Friends

When we call in the Guardians of the Quarters we are
inviting creatures that embody the qualities of these
Quarters to lend their energy and support to our magickal
workings. You don't have to physically see these creatures,
of course, or even intellectually believe in them, but one
of the secrets of effective magick is to learn how to treat
such beings as if they were real, living things in the Circle
with you. That might sound tricky but think back to your
childhood and you'll probably discover it's a talent you had
before you could spell your own name. I mean, remember those imaginary friends you had when you were really
little? Whether they existed or not, they felt real to you
and affected the way you saw and interacted with the
world.

Air – East – Sylphs (mythological creatures of air which float and look like beautiful wispy elven characters.)

Earth – South – Gnomes (mythological creatures which live and work in the earth. We all know what gnomes look like!)

Water – West – Undines (or Mermaids and Mermen, mythological creatures who live in oceans, rivers and streams.)

Fire – North – Salamanders (a type of amphibian/lizard with vibrant orange and black markings – because of this it became mythologised as a creature of fire.)

You are calling in these creatures because you are affirming the presence of the elements. There are others you can call in (some traditions use Angels or power animals, for example) but we will work with these for now.

HERE WE GO!

Make sure the space is as physically clean as possible: if it's your room, sweep or vacuum (yep, a good Teen Witch should be as handy with a Hoover as with a broom!).

Face the eastern quarter then, using your athame, pointed index finger of your power hand (your power finger) or wand, hold your arm out in front of you and turn in a sunwise (or deosil, which is anti-clockwise in the southern hemisphere) direction, visualising a stream of blue or diamond white light pouring out and forming a big circle around you as you turn.

POWER FINGER
The index finger of whatever hand you write with.

POWER HAND
The hand with which you write.

As you do this say:

> *I conjure you, (my/our) sacred Circle of power.*

When you get back to the start, picture the light spreading to form a sphere (or egg-like shape) above, below and all around you. Now, still facing east, hold your incense (or feather) in your power hand and fan it as you say:

> *Come, Guardians of Air,*
> *Bless (me/us) with your presence*
> *And magickal assistance.*

In your mind's eye take a moment to see the beautiful sylphs floating in that part of the Circle.

Now face North, hold up your candle or fire representation with your power hand and say:

Come, Guardians of the North,
Bless (me/us) with your presence
And magickal assistance.

In your mind's eye take a moment to see the salamanders writhe in, their bodies undulating like flames of fire.

Now face West, sprinkle a little water with your power hand and say:

Come, Guardians of the West,
Bless (me/us) with your presence
And magickal assistance.

In your mind's eye take a moment to see the lovely mermaids/mermen floating there.

Now face South and sprinkle a little salt/soil/sand with your power hand (or hold out your crystal) and say:

Come, Guardians of the South,
Bless (me/us) with your presence
And magickal assistance.

In your mind's eye take a moment to see the gnomes with their wise brown eyes gather there.

Now, facing your altar (or whatever you're using as one), raise both arms in the air and say:

(My/Our) Circle is empowered, bound and blessed.

Clap your hands once or strike your bell or gong and say firmly:

So Mote It Be.

At this point you will want to acknowledge the presence of the Lord and Lady. They are around all the time so you're not actually inviting them in – instead you are formally connecting with their energy inside you and your Circle.

Because a spell you may be casting might call for a specific Goddess or God (or both) to be invoked a bit later, at this point you are just honouring the divinity of creation.

Raise your arms and say:

Great Lady and Lord,
Below and Above
This Circle is filled
With your divine light and love.

Now you can do your ritual or spell.

Just a note: You might be working a particular spell that doesn't specify an incense or coloured candle to use. In that case when you are casting Circle use a stick of rosemary or frankincense incense or a feather for air. And just use a red or white candle for fire. If the spell you are using does require a certain incense and a special candle but you need to light them separatcly later on and not as a part of the Circle-casting ritual, then again, just use what I suggested above to cast Circle.

RAISING POWER

Raising power is something that is done in just about every spell-working. It is a way of creating lots of 'magickal fuel' to speed a spell on to fruition – in other words, give it a good kick start! Power raising is also used in healing rituals and anytime lots of oomph! is needed. There are masses of different methods and generally you raise the power inside Circle to allow it to brew up really strongly. Then, when it is peaking, you 'send' it to where it needs to go, by holding your athame or wand or power finger straight up in the air and visualising the top of the Circle opening up and the power racing away to do its job. Or you might point the athame (or wand, etc) at an object you are empowering (perhaps a talisman or amulet) and focus the energy into that.

Raising power is done to empower an amulet or object, or to fuel a spell that has been created within the circle. It's like getting in a car (the shell of the spell) and then turning the ignition on to power it up before driving away. Raising power is done any time it's needed.

WAYS TO RAISE POWER

Chanting is a good one – especially when you're sharing your Circle with a few other people. A classic Wiccan Goddess chant is excellent, 'Isis, Astarte, Diana, Hecate, Demeter, Kali, Inanna' but any relevant phrase repeated over and over can do the trick (there are some more suggestions in 'Top Teen Witch Tips'). This is another area where the TV Witches often miss the point – it's more often than not the intention behind the words that matters, not the words themselves. Stories where magic is unwittingly released by someone muttering the words in a spell book (like in the movie *The Mummy*, for instance) exist solely in fiction. In fact, power can be raised through wordless chant just as well as by using actual words.

Another method of raising power is to run around the perimeter of the Circle as you chant, either alone or in a group. When there's more than one of you in the Circle, hold hands and chant together until you feel it peak, then you can

either all raise your arms in the air and yell out 'So Mote It
Be' to send the energy on its way, or you can drop to the
ground and all press your hands into the earth or floor to
send the energy streaming along that way.

Another, quieter (!) way is to cup both hands together and
close your eyes, focusing on all the energy building up into a
supercharged energy ball in your hands. You'll feel it get
hotter and hotter and when it's absolutely peaking throw the
ball into the air to race off to its destination. A group can
also do this either individually or collectively – for example,
you can stand in a circle and hold your hands out to the
centre and manifest the ball together. You can change it to
be different colours if you like: blue for healing, pink for love,
purple for power – whatever!

When you are finished the energy-raising and directing part
of your ritual, eat and drink whatever goodies you brought
into the Circle with you to help you ground your energy (these
are called libations), saving some of both as an offering to
the Goddess and God. (If you are working outside, you can
crumble some food and pour drink on the ground or, if inside,
give it to a pot plant or save to take outside later.) A word of
warning: when I lived in a flat I used to pour my libations out
the window onto the garden and one night my downstairs
neighbour leant out the window at the wrong time and
copped some sticky grape juice square on his head! Which
was actually a kind of blessing – not that he saw it that way!

FINISHING UP

Now you can close down the Circle, which means you
need to acknowledge and thank the Lady, Lord and the
Guardians for their presence and assistance and disperse
the 'energy shield' of the Circle itself.

First acknowledge the Lord and Lady:

> *Lady and Lord,*
> *As above so below,*
> *To and from you*
> *All things flow.*

Now thank the Guardians of the Elements. Face East, fan your feather or incense and say:

> *Guardians of the Air,*
> *Hail and Farewell*
> *Until in Circle again we dwell.*

See the sylphs float away.

Face North, sprinkle some water and say:

> *Guardians of Fire,*
> *Hail and Farewell*
> *Until in Circle again we dwell.*

See the salamanders crawl away.

Face West, sprinkle some water and say:

> *Guardians of Water,*
> *Hail and Farewell*
> *Until in Circle again we dwell.*

See the mermaids/mermen swim away.

Face South, sprinkle a little salt/sand/soil or hold out your crystal, and say:

> *Guardians of Earth,*
> *Hail and Farewell*
> *Until in Circle again we dwell.*

And see the gnomes trundle off.

Just a note: You may have read in books that you need to call the Guardians deosil (anti-clockwise in the southern hemisphere) and farewell them widdershins (clockwise in the southern hemisphere). For this Circle casting it's fine for you to say hi and bye to them in a deosil direction.

Now hold out your athame, point your power finger

or wand and turn around in a widdershins direction (anti-sunwise/clockwise) and imagine light streaming out and cutting through the centre of the sphere, splitting it into two halves which start to turn into mist and disperse. As you do this, say:

> *This Circle is open but unbroken,*
> *Carried in (my/our) heart(/s);*
> *Always merry meet,*
> *Always merry part.*

Strike your bell, gong or clap your hands once to signal the end of the ceremony.

The 'always merry meet, always merry part' bit makes sense if there is a group of you because you are acknowledging that it is a joyous and empowering event to gather in Circle. If you are on your own 'always merry meet, always merry part' acknowledges the joy you feel in meeting with the Guardians and the formal presence of the Lady and Lord.

SUMMING IT UP

Remember! The main aim is to ease yourself into it, gradually mastering the full process, but be aware of these basic points:

 * You are creating a sacred space;
 * The four elements need to be formally acknowledged and the elemental Guardians called in;
 * The divinity of Creation needs to be acknowledged – that's why the Lady and Lord are honoured;
 * At the end you need to ground the magickal energy conjured up so you don't leave Circle feeling spaced out and uncomfortable. As well as grounding you, the food and libations (drink offered to the Lady and

Lord) acknowledge your connection with the earth and your understanding of the divine nature of all creation. You are the glue that holds all this together, so be clear and confident. The passion and belief you have in what you are doing will determine how cool your Circle is!

HOLD ON A MINUTE ...

You might say that if the above is enough to cast a Circle, why do I ever need to do anything more? Or if you've read my other books or any books on Witchcraft, you might be wondering, for example, 'What about stirring salt into the water?' or 'What about invoking and banishing pentagrams?' As I explained earlier, the Circle casting ritual above is a special one for Teen Witches that's easy to remember and will get you started. As you get more experienced and comfortable with the ritual, you will be drawn to more evocative and elaborate methods of Circle casting which will please and empower you more and reflect your growing capacities as a Witch. An analogy would be if this were a recipe book, the Circle casting above would be something nutritious, easy-to-prepare and filling, like scrambled eggs. Four-course banquets will come later as you become more acquainted with your skills. It's worth remembering that even cordon bleu chefs whip themselves up a quick and easy snack from time to time!

INSTANT CIRCLE OF PURE PROTECTION

For when you have no props!

When you have become adept at Circle casting and you have become familiar with the feeling that a well-cast

Circle provides, then you can begin casting Instant Circles of Pure Protection. But be aware that a real Instant Circle of Pure Protection can only be cast when you are adept at formal Circle casting.

Hold out your power finger and stretch out your arm to trace the blue/white Circle sphere in a deosil (anticlockwise) direction. As you do this say:

I conjure you, sacred Circle of power.

When you sense the glowing sphere around you, close your eyes, concentrate, raise your arms above your head and call in the elements:

Air – Earth – Water – Fire,
All the elements manifest,
So shall this Circle now be blessed.

Now honour the Lady and Lord, and, as you do this, sense the Circle filling with white light:

Lady and Lord,
As above so below,
To and from you
All things flow.

Now you have created a magick Circle which, depending on how strong your powers of visualisation are and how well you understand the full Circle casting ritual, will work just as well for simple spells and rituals.

To close this Circle, all you need to do is hold out your power finger, picture blue/white light pouring out and cut through the Circle boundary as you say:

The Circle is open but unbroken.

You don't need to farewell the elemental Guardians (as you didn't call them) or formally acknowledge the Lady and Lord again at this point as long as you are aware that you carry them in your heart.

TIPS FOR CREATING AN EFFECTIVE INSTANT CIRCLE OF PURE PROTECTION

✳ Really concentrate on the qualities of the elements.
✳ Feel air as you would feel the winds of the world rush around the planet, bringing new scents, new energies. Imagine it blowing your hair around, breathe in and out deeply and be aware of its role as a major life-giving force.
✳ Feel earth by visualising enormous mountains and earth-quakes splitting the surface to reveal layer upon layer of fertile damp soil. Sense your connection through the soles of your feet, making your energy one with that of the earth beneath you.
✳ Feel water by visualising the oceans of the world that carry so much life and form the majority of this planet's surface. The rivers, streams, lakes and seas are the blood of our planet, so feel your own salty blood course through your veins as you meditate on this element.
✳ Feel fire by picturing the explosive sun. Concentrate on the sensation of its heat on your face and also focus on the fiery molten core of our planet and its ability to create and destroy.

PURE POWER SHIELD
Snapping it on – Snapping it off

This is something you can do if you are feeling like you need a little protection from the outside world. Or you might want to create a mini sacred space whilst you mix up some herbs or read a book about the Craft.

Hold your power hand out to your side and snap your fingers three times as you say:

Perfect Power protects me,
One, two, three.

On the last snap see in your mind's eye a cord of blue light begin to whiz around you like a super-fast skipping rope. This will deflect any negative energy until you snap it off. To do this, stretch out your power hand again, snap your fingers three times and say:

Perfect Power switching off,
One, two, three, STOP!

See the blue cord disappear. I find you need to say 'stop' because as the blue light spins around you, it builds up to quite a strong intensity that just snapping your fingers doesn't always manage to earth. Saying 'stop' grounds any residue of energy properly. However, if you are feeling a bit jumpy after snapping your shield on and off, just press your hands onto the earth (or floor – whatever) and visualise any excess power draining back into the ground beneath you.

TEEN WITCH TOOLS OF THE TRADE

There are some basic tools that you will eventually want to have. However, some of you may not be allowed to own a large dagger (an athame) or light candles and incense in your room. So here is a list of things that can get you started and some important information about each:

Altar: The surface on which all your Witchy stuff lives. There are formal ways of setting up an altar, for example, certain coloured candles to be placed in

certain quarters. Your altar can be a little more like a
cross between an older Witch's altar and a collection
of gorgeous evocative Witchy stuff. Do keep it clean
and relatively uncluttered though. You might like to
have an altar cloth in a special colour like dark purple
or pale blue and maybe even embroidered or painted
with magickal symbols like suns, moons, stars,
pentagrams or sun/star signs. I don't have a cloth at
the moment – the one I've had for years is covered
with wax and scorched and I really have to get
around to cleaning it and giving it a facelift! So it's
rolled up right now and everything is just placed on
the clean white wooden surface of my little circular
altar. By the way, it's essential to keep your altar space
dedicated to your magic and keep it clear of half-
finished cups of tea, school text books and yesterday's
underwear!

Ideally your altar will be facing due South (the
Earth Quarter) but if your room's not nicely centred
on a North–South axis, just get as close to it as you
can. You will need to have the four elements
represented on your altar and if you know which way
it is facing you might like to put these in the same
quarters as you welcome the Guardians into Circle. So
you can have a bowl of water in the West, a candle
(new, red and unlit if you can't light flames in your
room) in the North, incense (or a feather) in the East,
and a bowl of salt/sand/soil or a crystal in the South.
(If you don't know the directions, don't worry – just
have these things placed somewhere on your altar,
though it's easy enough to buy a compass from a
good camping shop and get things nicely aligned.)

You will also want to have something that
represents the Lady and Lord, maybe little statues, or
pictures you've cut out from a magazine in frames,
even dressed up Barbie and Ken dolls! (Though not
even a Goddess could have a body like Barbie, it's
totally unnatural! And since the Lady and the Lord
represent the sacredness of life, creation and sexuality,
you might find Barbie and Ken's total lack of genitals
a little off-putting – still, if you can relate to them, go
ahead!) You just need something that represents the
Lady and Lord and their qualities strongly to you.

Also on your altar you could have some flowers or
a growing plant for nature and maybe some shells
you have collected to represent the ocean. As you
grow as a Teen Witch you will come across lots of
special things that you might like to place on your
altar, either permanently or for a little while. I tend
to have a lot of bits and pieces on my altar when I'm
not formally using it, which I then put to one side to
set up my altar more formally (and to make room for
ingredients for spells and things) when I am doing a
magickal ritual.

Athame – The Witch's dagger: Traditionally a
black-handled, double-bladed (but not sharp) knife
used to channel and focus energy. It is probably the
most unusual of a Witch's tools and has a certain
notoriety thanks to all those half-baked movies
where Witches are shown performing human
sacrifices with long, evil-looking knives. So some of
our younger readers oughtn't get too surprised if
their parents say: 'No way are you owning one of
those!' So, instead you can use your Power Finger to

substitute or you can use a wand. An athame is never used by a real Witch to cut anything solid and it should not be waved around to show off! It is one of the most sacred and personal things a Witch can own and needs to be treated with a lot of respect.

When placed on your altar, the athame is aligned with the element of Air.

Pentacle: This is a circular object that is usually made of clay or brass and has a pentagram (the sacred five-pointed star) marked on it. You can rest your athame on it, and it can also be used as a small plate to place your food on. It is aligned with the element of earth. A tip for making your own (cheap but effective) pentacle is to get a clay flower pot base (like a flat dish), turn it upside down and draw a pentagram on it (you could paint and decorate it in earthy colours like deep orange and brown).

Chalice: Basically a lovely glass or goblet used to hold your drink in. (There is another use for the chalice in older Witches' circle casting and ritual which is mentioned in my other books, but for Teen Witches, it's best as a drinking vessel.) It is aligned with the element of water and can be crystal, glass, metal – but it must only be used during magickal work.

Wand: Everyone knows what a wand is! It can channel and focus energy and help conjure things into being. You can make your own: an easy one to make in Australia is to find a nice straight gum tree branch about 45 cm long and as thick as your thumb or index finger. (If you absolutely have to cut it from a tree, ask for permission first and give thanks after.)

Strip the leaves and twigs off it and sand it down until smooth. You can whittle both ends to a blunt point or bind a crystal (perhaps clear quartz or amethyst) to one end with a cloth or leather cord. If you like decorate the wand by painting meaningful symbols (perhaps some runes).

A wand is aligned with the element of fire.

Bell (or gong): You can use a bell or gong to ring in and seal the Circle or to signify the beginning or end of a ritual or ceremony. You don't need to have one – you can clap your hands instead – but I think it adds a nice touch!

Incense: This represents the element of air and can be substituted with a feather (if you can't have a flame in your room). Different scents represent various physical and metaphysical qualities. Incense can be burnt as sticks or cones, but I prefer using charcoal discs and sprinkling powdered incense on top. You have to make sure when using the discs that they rest on sand or similar since they get *very* hot. And make sure you put them out with some water or bury them in the sand when you're finished. *Never* leave one unattended! A good tip for getting the best, purest scent from powdered incense is to place a small piece of alfoil on top of the burning disc and place your incense on that. Not as much smoke is created, the incense burns longer and all you need to do is give it a little stir with a twig or similar occasionally to keep it cooking.

Candles: Aligned with the element of fire whether they're lit or unlit. Different colours have different magickal meanings and abilities. You will probably have at least a couple of candles on your altar – you might have little tea lights to shine some light on the proceedings (since working by everyday, household electric lights is a great way to make a Circle fizzle) and taller, coloured candles which are a part of specific spells or rituals. My altar is covered in candles. I have two, one in a sun base and one in a moon base, to represent the Lord and Lady (God and Goddess); a big fat white one that is my 'light' so I can see what I'm doing; a red one in the fire quarter to formally represent the element of fire; and then I usually have a special coloured one that has been anointed in magickal oils which is part of a spell I'm doing.

Bowl of water: To represent the element of water, of course! The bowl can be glass, pottery or even a large sea shell.

Crystals: I usually have a couple on my altar to help intensify magickal energies or for me to hold when I'm raising power or visualizing. Amethyst and fluorite are my faves at the moment. Crystals are aligned with the element of earth.

Cauldron: Another notorious Witchy accessory! I have left this for last – it's not essential and a good cauldron can be quite expensive. If you are part of a Teen Witch Coven, you might like to all pitch in and buy one together. The cauldron is very symbolic, representing the fertile womb of the Great Mother, from which all things come and to which all return. A cauldron can be used to brew magickal potions in (edible and inedible!). It can also hold fire and be used to burn offerings or paper petitions.

Mortar and Pestle: A handy bowl and stick to grind up incenses and powders. You can find them at any good cooking supply store. I bought mine at an Indian supermarket (where they're used to grind up all the spices used in Indian cooking).

BOOK OF SHADOWS

I'm sure that those of you at school or university will have more than enough books cluttering up your lives. But a Book of Shadows is really important for a Teen Witch. You are going to be learning a lot at this point of your Witchy life and you will benefit by keeping track of what you're doing. Apart from anything else, it will be fun to look back on as a wise old Witch and see how far you've come!

A Teen Witch Book of Shadows doesn't have to be a big deal (though it can be if you want!). It can even be on your computer though make sure you back it up on a floppy. However, I think pen (or ink, crayon, coloured pencil – whatever!) and paper is ultimately more rewarding. You could have a folder with plastic pocket inserts to slip in left-over packets of incense you used or created, or a special feather you used for a particular ritual, Polaroids you took of a gathering you had, a tape of you chanting – anything! At the very least your Book of Shadows should have notes on what you did, the results and any insights from along the way.

While a personal Book of Shadows is a must, some Wiccan traditions also have more formalised books of shared material, and if you are initiated into a Coven as an adult Witch you might need to copy their Book of Shadows by hand – primarily to help you learn and absorb Coven knowledge and experience.

If you are part of a Teen Witch Coven, it's a good idea for at least someone to keep a record of what you're all doing as a group. Perhaps you could take turns and have each member contribute different insights into the rituals and spells you work.

Hot Spell Tips

Here are some ideas for you to get the most out of your spell-casting.

INSTANT PERSONAL BLESSING

As a young Catholic, I used to make the 'sign of the cross' before entering Church or after communion, and now, as a Witch, I make the sign of the pentagram as a quick mini-ritual of self-blessing and protection. I find this helps me focus and strengthen my Witchy powers.

First touch your third eye, then your right nipple, left shoulder, right shoulder, left nipple and then third eye again, to trace out the sacred five-pointed star.

EMPOWER YOUR INGREDIENTS

Before you start any spell or ritual it's good to cleanse

and empower what you're working with. After casting
Circle hold your hands over your altar and the ingredients,
like the herbs or objects you are using. Take a moment to
close your eyes and inhale deeply. Feel the palms of your
hands tingle and grow hot as you focus your energy there.
When you are ready, in your mind's eye see pure white
light streaming from your hands and into the objects as
you say:

> *I cleanse these objects of negativity*
> *With light that's pure and positive.*
> *I empower these objects to work my will*
> *For the good of all and with harm to none.*

WHEN SPELLCASTING . . .

Believe that your magick will work and fuel it with your
passion and intent. Try not to cast spells when you're feeling
really sad or angry unless you feel very confident about
being able to channel these emotions as fuel for your workings. If you're feeling scattered or vague, wait until you feel
clearer. You could try a candle meditation to clear your
head.

Memorise the incantations: it might be a hassle,
but trust me, it's worth it. When you know the words
and you're not looking at a book, you can really
focus on the energies you are conjuring.

Part of my television work involves me memorising long
spiels to say to camera. I used to look at the paragraphs in
front of me and think, 'Oh my Goddess, how am I going
to remember all this?' But gradually, after repeating line by
line, it would sink in. Then I got really good at it (mem-

orising is an art you can learn) and now I can memorise long passages with no trouble. And usually it's stuff I'm not that personally attached to! When I'm memorising things that I'm absolutely passionate about, like incantations and invocations, learning things off by heart is a pleasure!

Be resourceful: you may not have the right coloured candle, or it may be the waning moon and the spell says to do it on a waxing moon. Do the spell anyway. In my first and second books there are hints on substitution, but here are a few suggestions:

* A white candle can replace any other candle except black.
* You can substitute herbs by understanding what they are used for and finding ones with similar qualities. If I don't have an unusual herb I find lavender is easily attainable and a good substitute for just about everything as it has great transformative and nurturing qualities, and can effectively charge up just about any spell.

Research: when you need to invoke a Goddess or God for a spell, make sure you know what you are welcoming. Do some research, so that you know exactly where they're coming from and what their primary energies are. Don't just call in a name, call in a presence.

SPELL SEALING CHARM

Unless there is a specific suggestion for a spell ending, it's a good idea to seal it off with this:

This I ask for the good of all
So that harm may come to none,
So Mote it Be,
My will be done.

MAGICKAL MEDITATIONS

A lot of the symbolism in spell working and ritual needs to be charged up by the powers of your mind's eye and your emotions. There are simple things you can do to improve your powers of visualisation and psychic abilities.

To improve my overall powers of visualisation, I like colouring in landscapes – I let my eyes relax and I start to change the colour of leaves on a tree from green to pink. I see the colour change as if the tip of the leaf has been dipped into a pool of pink water and is absorbing it like a sponge. You'll be amazed at how quickly you can master this. Of course, in the physical world the leaves aren't changing into pink, but in the reality I have created they are.

There is another fun visualisation practice that I call 'Rubbing it Out'. If I am waiting for a taxi or whatever, I will focus on a distant building (city skylines are good) and start 'rubbing it out' as if I have a giant eraser. I will do this until I can visualise the skyline minus the building I have rubbed out. (If you find that the buildings are actually getting demolished in real life while you're doing this, you're obviously too good – stop it immediately!)

Another good discipline to develop psychic powers is the Candle Meditation. Light a candle in a dark room and gaze at the flame. When you are ready, try to make it flicker to the left and right at your will. See if you can make the

flame grow long and short at your will. Keep playing with
the flame until you have mastered its movements. Now,
you might think this sounds impossible – but try it out, I
dare you! It's likely you'll be amazed at the results!

THE MAGICK OF LIFE

People can get hung up on the Hollywood hocus pocus
results of spellcasting. They expect results like the ones the
girls from *Charmed* get. But real magick is far more profound than this: if life was like *Sabrina* or *Charmed* everyone would take it for granted and we would become
bored, demanding and out of synch with the tidal ebbs and
flows of life.

When we understand and contemplate the interconnectedness of all things, then we see that the 'special effects'
witchcraft of movies and TV is not as exciting and moving
as real, natural magick. However, anything's possible. Don't
forget that only eighty years ago if someone had said there
would be a small box sitting in the corner of your living
room in which people could talk and move around in different environments, they would have thought you were
insane. Of course, we now know that box as a television!

Even science (especially the field of quantum physics)
is now explaining what Witches have known instinctively
all along: what we imagine to happen can and will – we
can affect reality by the strength and passion of our minds
(not just by snapping our fingers!). And when we become
adept at harnessing and focusing the elemental powers as
well and start making magick, anything is possible!

A Witch's Sacred Days

Sabbats are the eight seasonal festivals celebrated by Witches (think Christmas and Easter but a lot more often!) which correspond with both traditional agricultural events (like the sowing and harvesting of crops, and seasonal changes) and astronomical events – the solstices and equinoxes. We celebrate the Sabbats as a way of keeping ourselves attuned to the cycles of life as they come and go outside us and within us.

The four major (agriculturally-based) Sabbats are Samhain, Imbolc, Beltane and Lammas, and the four minor (astronomically-based) Sabbats are Yule, Ostara, Litha and Mabon.

The Wheel of the Year is the name of this cycle of festivals and the Wheel of the Year Myth is the story that enhances our understanding and insight into these sacred times. (See *Witch – A Magickal Year* to find out more).

I have discussed the Sabbats at length in both my previous books, but here I would like to offer some simple, enjoyable and empowering ways that Teen Witches can honour and celebrate these sacred times and the turning of the Wheel of the Year in a unique and easy way. The suggestions below can be incorporated into a party-like gathering, a small meeting of one or two people, or as a solo experience.

While Teen Witches can celebrate the eight Sabbats, many of you will most likely still be expected to (and want to!) celebrate the Christmas and Easter holidays. This is fine – just be aware of the ancient origins of these celebrations and the underlying fact that they are about love and sharing good times together.

SAMHAIN
May 1 (Southern Hemisphere)
October 31 (Northern Hemisphere)

Samhain is a time to remember our ancestors. Get together with your Witchy friends and each bring a photo of a loved one (or loved ones) who has passed on and share your favourite memories of them. Dress in black and burn patchouli and myrrh incense to honour their spirits. This festival has been commercialised as Halloween and is marketed as a time to go 'trick or treating' and scaring each other. However, as long as you remain aware that it is also a special time to respect the dead, you can have a bit of fun with Halloween props like jack o' lanterns and pointy hats and broomsticks! Even the most serious Wiccan festivals should still be fun.

YULE
June 20–23 (Southern Hemisphere)
December 20–23 (Northern Hemisphere)
(depending on the actual day of the solstice)

Suggest that everyone bathe in chamomile (pour a cup of the tea into the bath) before dressing in reds and purples. Gather together for a bonfire, (or a fire in an open fireplace at someone's home). Tonight you will be celebrating the longest night of the year, and at sunrise it is the beginning of the ascent of the sun – from now on the days will be longer and get warmer. The journey towards spring has begun.

Get the fire going and place the Yule log in the centre. Traditionally the Yule log is oak, but I have used gum tree wood and decorated it with gold and red ribbons. As it burns, I sprinkle myrrh and frankincense resin on it. You can also throw on handfuls of gum leaves and make wishes as the smoke swirls towards the newborn sun, which will catch them and infuse them with its growing life force.

Have a big feast of your favourite winter foods, like soups and casseroles and puddings, and drink warm, honey-spiced grape juice. If you are allowed to sit up all night to welcome the sun in, do so! As it rises, everyone can light a red candle from the sparks of the Yule log in honour of the new sun/son. Everyone can also take home some of the charred Yule log in a little green bag tied with gold ribbon. Put this under your bed to ensure a safe and happy home.

IMBOLC
August 1 (Southern Hemisphere)
February 2 (Northern Hemisphere)

New beginnings and new inspirations are to be experienced during Imbolc. Do a big cleanout of your room and get rid of anything you don't need anymore. Have a gathering where everyone writes a list of things that they want to achieve by the next Sabbat (Ostara is seven weeks away) and then turn it into a poem. All wear white and should bring a white candle and flower to the gathering.

Stand in a circle and read out your poems and then together ask the Goddess to bless your goals. Raise energy by holding hands and chanting Goddess names, 'Isis, Astarte, Diana, Hecate, Demeter, Kali, Inanna' and when the power peaks, throw your hands in the air and shout: 'May all our dreams come true!' Have a feast featuring pasta with pesto (basil, one of the main ingredients, is a sacred herb at this time). Wrap your poem around a bay leaf and keep it on your altar or in your Book of Shadows. Now is also a good time to buy a new pentagram necklace (if you wear one).

OSTARA
September 20–23 (Southern Hemisphere)
March 20–23 (Northern Hemisphere)
(depending on the actual day of the equinox)

Ostara is the Witches' Easter – it's a time to celebrate that spring is here and the land is alive and regenerating. Get dressed up in gorgeous colourful clothing, put flowers in your hair, get everyone together and go for a picnic. Chocolate Easter eggs that you saved from the commercial Easter can be eaten now! (That's if you managed to save them, which is one of the ultimate tests of a Teen Witch's self-discipline!). You can also decorate real eggs – painting them with symbols meaningful to you and placing them on your altar.

BELTANE
October 31 (Southern Hemisphere)
May 1 (Northern Hemisphere)

Beltane is the Fertility festival: a time to honour creation itself. Choose a beautiful natural setting and make a big circle of ivy to sit in. Feast on lots of fresh fruits like strawberries and apples – luscious, succulent things. Talk openly about your feelings and affection for the important people in your life. Share a loving cup (all take a sip from one cup) and pass a kiss around from one to the other as an open expression of unconditional love. Each person should bring a passage to read from a book or a poem that inspires their passion and reverence for life to share with everyone else.

LITHA
December 20–23 (Southern Hemisphere)
June 20–23 (Northern Hemisphere)
(depending on the actual solstice)

Litha is the longest day of the year and the time the sun is at its peak. From now on the days will gradually grow shorter and the descent towards Winter has begun (even though, in Australia, we are about to hit our hottest weather). It is traditional at this time to throw lavender on a fire to ensure safety for the coming year – but mostly everywhere will have a fire ban! Instead, burn lavender incense and scatter rose petals around your feasting table. Have a dinner early in the warm evening and enjoy the balmy weather. As this is the commercial Christmas time, you could bond with that energy and exchange gifts of opulence like richly scented incense and candles, lucky coins and amulets. (While some Witches save the present-giving business for our own Yule festival, a lot of us like any excuse to share gifts with those we love and are more than happy to do so at Litha as well as Yule. Shopkeepers love us!)

LAMMAS
February 2 (Southern Hemisphere)
August 1 (Northern Hemisphere)

Lammas is a time to honour the harvest, not only of the land but of the rewards reaped for our hard work in all areas of our lives. Gather together and bake bread with sunflower seeds, being aware of how the combining of skills can create new opportunities. As you are feasting on the freshly baked bread, make sure to offer some to the Goddess and God. Together, trade stories of your successes and share insights you have achieved over the last year.

MABON
March 20–23 (Southern Hemisphere)
September 20–23 (Northern Hemisphere)
(depending on the actual date
of the equinox)

Mabon is the final harvest of crops before winter, and is a wonderful time to look back over the past year and at what you have achieved. Write down what you feel most proud of and throw the paper into a fire with a handful of sage as an offering to the Goddess and God, asking them to bless and acknowledge your efforts.

THE ESBAT

Another important time for Witches to gather together is every Full Moon – this is a potent time for magick of all sorts and a very appropriate time to honour the Goddess at her most visible. The occasion is also often celebrated by a beautiful traditional ritual called 'Drawing Down the Moon' where the Priestess of a Coven will draw down the Lunar Essence to empower and bless the Coven.

I tend to be fairly spontaneous when honouring and celebrating the Full Moon, but I always do something. Maybe I will go outside and gaze at her full face as she rises over the horizon and do some chanting. At other times I may do a full-blown ritual involving casting Circle and reciting the 'Charge of the Goddess' to draw down the energy (see Witch – A Personal Year for the Charge of the Goddess.).

While writing this book I was lucky enough to experience an extraordinary full lunar eclipse. I was staying in a beautiful mountain country house with gorgeous landscaped gardens and natural bush settings, and on the night of the eclipse it was extremely cold with not a cloud in the sky.

With two friends I watched the moon rise blindingly white from a clearing in the bush. Gradually, the shadow of the Earth softened the moon's glow until it took on a rosy hue. We stood spellbound as the moon became a soft pink pearl floating in the sky. At this point I cast Circle around the fire we had lit and I said the 'Charge of the Goddess' in honour of this special night, and then we each threw handfuls of lavender into the fire and made wishes. As the smoke swirled into the sky in offering to the Goddess, we knew our wishes would come true.

It was a truly magickal night and we stayed out for hours until the fire had burnt down and the moon had returned to a beaming white orb.

It is appropriate for Teen Witches to create their own meaningful ritual for the Full Moon, leaving formal 'Drawing Down the Moon' rituals until you are a little further down the path of your Craft. Rituals that you create yourself, with full awareness of the process involved will be more magickal and honour the Goddess more than something complicated you get out of a book and, perhaps don't fully understand. So light candles, sing songs, make wishes and give thanks for all the good things in life knowing that the Goddess is smiling down upon you.

It's Only Natural

When I was writing this book I was extremely lucky to stay at a beautiful country home in Mount Macedon, Victoria. Mount Macedon is right next to Hanging Rock, the beautiful and eerie place that is the setting for the story of the disappearance of four schoolgirls in 1900, immortalised by Joan Lindsay in her novel *Picnic at Hanging Rock*. It is a magickal area, incredibly lush and fertile, even in the winter months. Since Witchcraft is a nature-worshipping religion, I couldn't imagine a better place to write a book for budding Teen Witches. Each day I would take long walks all rugged up in the cold air and just allow the awesome natural beauty around me to seep into my consciousness and make me feel at one with myself and the world.

Alone I would stop and listen to the silence. Of course, it was never completely silent – I could hear the rustle of grass and bushes, the sweet calls of birds, the hushed roar of the wind as it whisked across the tops of the huge gum trees. My work is often very demanding and sees me in hectic urban environments and crowded smoky nightclubs and venues, which can stress me out and leave me feeling really depleted. So being away from cars, radios, people's voices, machines and clutter was enormously healing and put me in touch more than ever with the ultimate meaning of being a Witch.

I sometimes wandered off the dirt road into the bush. I would just keep going, clambering over mossy rocks and fallen logs and gurgling waterways that had formed after the heavy rain the night before. Thick piles of composting, russet red leaves would squish under foot as I made my way deeper into the magickal weave of giant, glowing green ferns and tangled twigs and branches of shrubs and bushes. I sipped rainwater that had pooled on big flat leaves and stopped when I sensed it was right to and just breathe and listen. Once I was sure I could hear the groaning of a giant red-barked gum as its twisted trunk eased its way up out of the ground through the canopy until its leaves nestled high in the grey mist above. I meditated on that spiralling trunk, seeing in it the spirals of life and nature – a DNA coil, the cone of a sea shell, incense smoke released with flame, the swirl of light I see in a Cone of Power raised in Circle.

I went for a walk one morning after a long night of writing – my eyes were tired and I had switched on my computer but something just made me get up and leave its blank, blue screen and walk outside. I descended the long driveway looking up at the towering gums, feeling the cold air on my cheeks and the lightest mist of rain on my face. As I took a few more slow steps, my gaze travelled across to the mesh of dripping green leaves of a giant fern, my feet crunching on the gravel. Then I felt the impulse to look up again. Perched in the high fork of a gum tree sat a koala looking at me sleepily. The branches she was nestled in held her like a cradle, rocked by the wind. We watched each other for a while with her occasionally looking away to observe the oncoming misty clouds that floated across the top of the mountain. Every now and again a stronger blast of wind would come: 'Hang on!', I laughed, as I watched her sway wildly back and forth. As she craned her neck I could see a fluffy, white fur collar under her chin that contrasted with her short, sleek grey body fur. Eventually she stretched, turned around and started to make her way further up the slim trunk, her big black claws gripping effortlessly. Perched higher, she lazily reached out to grab some gum leaves to munch on. It was the first time I had seen a wild koala and I was overwhelmed standing there, a lone human sharing this beautiful animal's space.

It never ceases to amaze me how it is so easy to get caught up in the extreme stress and stimulation of living in an urban environment, so much so that you lose the innate sense of peace that we all have a right to feel. Even after all my years as a Witch I still get caught up pushing myself to do more and more, trying to get to a point where I feel satisfied with my efforts. I do this because the pressure of city life cuts me off from a rewarding sense of self and I get tricked into thinking that by 'doing' I will reach that point of fulfilment. However, the answer doesn't lie in 'doing' but in 'being' – just stopping, and being in the moment. Then everything is enough.

So, if you are ever feeling really cut off from enjoying life and nothing you do seems enough, take yourself off into the country, or a lush park or open beach, and let your mind wander and breathe deeply. Connect with your natural self – this is one of the best Witchy disciplines I can suggest.

There are many spells and rituals you can do working with natural energy and objects – you're only limited by your imagination. Often the more remote and untouched your environment is, the more natural magick there is to be tapped into. Remember – you don't have to cast Circle for these, but can if you like, although you are already in a naturally sacred space, perfect for these spells and rituals.

RIVER BLESSING

Follow a flowing stream or river, observing its methods and sharing its space. When I do this, I reflect on the beauty of the moving water and imagine what it would feel like to be water spilling over rocks, swirling in pools and rushing through channels. I focus on feeling my blood moving through my veins and connect with how, in a small way, my body reflects the great waterways of the planet.

To honour and to receive a blessing of the stream or river, it is appropriate to perform the Pentagram Salute. Dip your index finger in the cascading water and trace from third eye (the space between your eyebrows) to right nipple to left shoulder across to right shoulder to left nipple and back to third eye.

TREE THOUGHTS

Let yourself be drawn to a tree. You might be attracted to a lush and beautiful young fig tree or you might be drawn to the old, gnarled, textured branches of a gum. Kneel at

your chosen tree's base and offer your respect. Meditate on the absolute magnificence of trees and become aware of their essential and amazing presence on this planet, yet they are so taken for granted. When you are ready, leave something of yourself as an offering (like a lock of your hair or a kiss bestowed on the tree's trunk) and join a conservation group if you are not already a part of one.

BIRD CALL DIVINATION

Ask a question and wait to hear a bird call: one means no, two means yes, three means ask again, and silence means the outcome is unclear or that it is better for you not to be certain at this point. A whole cacophony of birdsong means everything you desire will come to you!

FLOWER DIVINATION

This works very well with roses, but any flower in bud can be used. Gently tie a small white ribbon around the stem of one bud and a small blue one around the other. Then make yourself known to the plant by saying:

I respectfully ask, oh flower divine,
To reveal the answer to this question of mine.

Pour an offering of spring water on its roots and ask your question. If the white ribbon full blooms first, the answer is yes; if the blue, the answer is no.

It's worth noting you need to ask really straightforward questions where a yes/no answer will suffice. You need to do this spell using only one species of plant as some bloom faster than others, but rather than tying ribbons you could choose two plants of the same species whose flowers are different colours. Decide which colour will be 'yes' and which 'no'.

EARTH DIVINATION

Go somewhere where there is lots of cracked dried earth. I like doing this at the beach on a very hot day where the top layer of sand has become baked and has separated into a latticework of patterns. Using a stick, trace a metre diameter circle in a deosil (sunwise/anticlockwise) direction and as you do chant:

Circle of earth revealing
Scenes of my future being.

Now sit and gaze at the patterns formed by the cracked sand (or earth). Ask a question and allow your eyes to go out of focus and your subconscious to open up. You will be amazed at what is revealed. You might see pictures form in the sand or words might just float into your head. When you are finished, open the circle by tracing back over it in a widdershins/clockwise direction.

RIVER SPELL

This is for when you've been having a hard time and you want to move on.

Go to a flowing river at sunrise. Hold a stick in your hand and focus all the thoughts of things you want to let go of into the stick. When you are ready cast it into the river and watch it float away as you say:

> *As the river flows, I let go*
> *Yesterday, its story told;*
> *I go forth wise and bold*
> *As another day unfolds.*

Turn around and walk away without looking back.

STONE SPELL

Stones are wonderful for absorbing problems that need to be dealt with. This is a banishing ritual that works wonders. Choose a soft stone that you can mark with another, harder stone. Focus on what you want to get rid of – it might be a bad habit like biting your nails, overeating, irrational fear of something, or even a person who is giving you grief and you want them to stop bugging you. As you do this, dig a hole in the earth at least 20 cm deep.

When you have a very clear image carve either the name of the thing or a symbol that represents it (for example, you might draw fear as a big 'X' – just make sure your symbol is meaningful to you and allow your intuition to choose it). When you have done this, hold the stone in both hands and say:

> *Begone, begone, begone from me,*
> *I cast away and bury deep*

That which no longer works for me,
With harm to none So Mote It Be.

Drop the stone into the hole and cover it up. Walk away
without looking back. You can also do this at the ocean's
edge or, better yet, standing on a cliff over the ocean and
throwing the stone into the water. You can do this spell as
often as necessary – depending on your power of visualisation and focus you might need to repeat it a few times.
To maximise effectiveness, try to perform this spell during
the waning moon and for even more oomph! on a Saturday.

CHANTING

I often chant when I am alone in nature and I recommend
it to you! I usually do either the classic Wiccan Goddess
Chant: 'Isis, Astarte, Diana, Hecate, Demeter, Kali, Inanna'
or an old Sanskrit chant my yoga teacher gave me – unfortunately there's no way I could work out the spelling of it
to print here!

When I chant to honour nature, I focus on how the
sounds emanating from my natural instrument, my voice,
blend and weave with nature's instruments around me.
Leaves rustling together, branches rubbing and creaking in
the wind, water cascading over stones or falling as droplets
into a pond. Birds and animals vocalise along too – all sounds
seem to speak to me, centre me and share their wisdom.

An important practice of Aboriginal spirituality is
'singing to the land'. It honours and reinforces our ties to
the land. Even those of us who are white are not indigenous and are not initiated into ancient Aboriginal traditions and songs, we can honour our unique and divine land
spirit by offering our own songs and hearts.

FIRE MEDITATION

There's nothing quite like sitting outside at night and staring into the dancing flames and glowing, shimmering coals of an open fire. Fire like this encourage contemplation and insight (a friend of mine calls it 'Aboriginal TV'!). I like to do smoke divination by throwing gum leaves on the fire and looking for pictures and images in the heavy swirling smoke. An effective magick ritual is to write your wishes and hopes on little pieces of coloured paper (check out the colour correspondences in 'Hot Spell Tips') and throw them into the fire so that its energy will help make them come true. Remember though – always check fire regulations, and whether there is a ban in place first (usually this is in summer).

FAERIES AND NATURE SPIRITS

According to one theory, the original faeries were the pre-Celtic Pagan peoples of the British Isles, France and Germany. Evidence of this can be seen in both custom and language – for example, one of the races living in Britain before the Celts was the Picts, which is almost certainly the source of the word 'Pixie'. The skeletal remains of members of these races show that they tended to be smaller and more lithe in build than subsequent arrivals to these regions, hence the notion of the faerie as being the Little People. They lived in harmony with the natural cycles of the land and, when driven into hiding by later contenders for the land, they gradually became mythologised as mysterious inhabitants of the wild country, possessed of supernatural powers gained through their adherence to the oldest religion.

The Irish still believe the faerie folk or 'Sidhe' live in the hills of Ireland in burial grounds and graves and emerge at certain times of the year (during festivals like Samhain). For the majority of people now, however, faeries are pop- ularised as gorgeous little winged creatures that bestow blessings and good fortune, and a complicated and elabo- rate mythological world full of different types of faerie folk has evolved.

Whatever their origins, faeries are also often considered to be spirits of nature, which is how I related to them as a child – subtle beings living not only close to the land, but inside it. When I was younger I used to make homes for faeries in the bush. I would fashion stones, twigs, moss and flower petals into little abodes at the base of a shrub or under the big, flat exposed root of a tree. While writing this book I would often sit next to a small waterfall, and as I became mesmerised by the silky, dancing water, I could swear I saw sparkling little creatures hopping from rock to rock, splashing through the thin sheets of water.

The way to see faeries is to open your heart to the pos- sibility that they exist and fuel that with wonder and love. Better yet, create your own garden and invite them to share it with you. If you can, have a small part of your yard all to yourself (or if you live in a flat, planter boxes and pots of your own). Make sure your garden is fertilised organically – which means no artificial chemicals or pesticides! Talk to your plants and let them know you love them. Grow and nurture lots of coloured flowers and scented herbs – faeries love these! Breathing in the scent of flowers and herbs is also healing for the human soul: my favourites are gardenias, camellias, roses, jasmine, tiger lilies, lavender, rosemary and basil. Stud the soil around your plants with crystals and shells and tie coloured ribbons on stems and branches to attract faeries. You can write wishes and goals on the ribbons with a silver pen and ask the faeries to help make them come true.

Parents – Can't Live With Them, Can't Live Without Them!

I have a great relationship with Mum and Dad now but getting to that point took a while. It probably wasn't until my mid-twenties that we really started to become good friends and put the difficult times of my teens behind us.

Yes, I had a very tumultuous time growing up with my parents. And when I hit my teens all hell broke loose! I am the oldest child, so as I was finding my feet as a human being, my parents were finding their feet as parents. Unsurprisingly, we all made lots of mistakes! From when I was as young as twelve, there were many times when all I wanted to do was run away – and I would. I would pinch some biscuits from the pantry, get a bottle of cordial and my toothbrush and set off. I don't think I was seriously intending to run away, more just searching for some attention and trying to get my parents to understand how desperately unhappy I was. I would start walking through the bush but never go much further than a few kilometres before I would turn around and go home and sneak the stuff back into the pantry, leaving my parents none the wiser. I really felt I didn't want to be there, but I couldn't really leave.

I guess being adopted didn't help. It's very easy to feel alienated from your parents as a teen, and add to this all the adoption issues and it's extra trouble. I remember when I was fourteen or so being at one of the big family Christmas gatherings where everyone would get together to celebrate the season of peace and goodwill by spending most of the day gossiping about each other. One of my relatives came up to me and said, 'Your mother will never love you as much as I love my children, because you're not really hers. You're not really anyone's, are you?' This was not very helpful and nurturing for a neurotic fourteen-year-old!

It often seemed that I had nothing in common with Mum and Dad. We argued over *everything*. To make matters worse, my parents held on to the attitude they experienced themselves as kids of 'spare the rod and spoil the child', i.e. lots of punishment. The rift between us grew larger and larger and one of the strongest memories of my teens (and why I decided to move out at fifteen) is of crying myself to sleep every night.

I know my parents were doing the best they knew how and that their own upbringing dictated how they raised me. I was very opinionated and headstrong, but even then I could sometimes be a bit too easily led and tended to fall in with the 'wrong' groups at school. I'm the first to admit that I must have been a handful for my parents.

Funnily enough, one of the things that started me on the path of Witchcraft was rebelling against my parents by not eating what they did! Mum used to put salt on everything, so I started to refuse to use salt. Mum and Dad ate meat, so I decided to become a vegetarian. This was very hard because Mum would insist that I ate like the rest of the family, but if I managed not to eat everything on my plate I felt I had succeeded in defying them. Out of this I started to become aware of vegetarianism and healthy eating which, although now common, was something people associated with hippies and the Hare Krishnas.

As I have mentioned, I only started practising Witchcraft in my late teens, so what would I have done differently if I had been a Teen Witch from an earlier age?

For a start I would have been a lot more forgiving and tolerant of my parents. I would have realised that the harsh injustices they seemed to be heaping on me were a reflection of their own childhoods and they were trying to protect me from harm and misfortune. I would have been more appreciative of how hard Dad worked to keep three kids clothed, fed, healthy, educated and with a roof over our heads. I would have been more connected with my mother's challenge of raising three kids of different ages, all having different 'mothering' needs.

The wonderful thing about the Craft is that it heightens your sense of personal power, whatever age you begin practising it. When you're a teenager you can sometimes feel extremely disempowered by your home life and take every opportunity to rebel just to give you a sense of your own power. But as a Teen Witch the important thing to focus on is realising all the power you will ever need is inside you and then it doesn't become an issue to prove it to yourself and others. For example, a real martial arts expert feels no need to pick fights for fun, so a talented Teen Witch doesn't need to create all the battlefields other kids require as a testing ground.

I also would have tried not to have taken things so personally and letting situations get out of control. I remember one thing my father used to say to me would always make me furious: after giving me some kind of ultimatum, like not letting me go to a school dance, he would refuse to explain his reasons. He would say, 'You don't need to know why – your opinion doesn't matter. Just do as you're told.' I would slip into autopilot and keep pushing, saying, 'Tell me – it's so unfair, why can't I go?', only to have him repeat the same – that my opinion wasn't the issue, that I asked too many questions and so on and so on. In the end it would be a screaming match . . . And I would still not be allowed to go to the school dance.

I would go to my room or run out into the bush, sit there and cry, hate my parents, hate my life and, worst of all, hate myself. I would take everything he said inside me and let it fester like a cancer undermining any sense of security or personal worth I might have had – which is one of the things the Craft strengthens with every Circle or spell you ever do.

This carried over into other areas of my life, and made my behaviour worse as I attempted to compensate for the lack I felt deep inside by doing stupid things to try to impress the cool kids at school. Naturally that would just get me in more trouble, get me grounded more often and on it would go.

Some of my friends at school had great relationships with their parents – well, they thought it was great. One girl was allowed to do pretty much whatever she liked. She only had her mum (her dad had left them when she was very young) and she was an only child. Looking back now I think her mum let her do anything because she felt guilty there wasn't a father around. This had good and bad effects. She could go out as late as she liked, she could have boyfriends and friends over, she could say what she liked, swear her head off, and when she was fourteen she was even allowed to smoke. Basically her mother didn't say 'Boo' to her and the girl thought it was great. However, in the end, she was given too much rope and ultimately hanged herself with it. She didn't do well at school, not because she couldn't but because she never studied or did her homework since her mother never forced the issue with her. She could also get her mum to write her sick notes for days off school and spent her free time at the local shopping centre where she took up stealing cosmetics – and eventually got busted for it. Her smoking gave her acne and by the age of fifteen she was pregnant to one of the boys that her mother used to let her hang out and drink alcohol in the loungeroom with.

What a mess. Sadly, she never really cleaned up her act. She miscarried the baby, but was soon pregnant again. She dropped out of school, and then at seventeen married the father of her baby who turned out to be a violent drug addict who beat her up. She is now divorced and has kids to two different fathers, lives in a housing commission flat and is on a single mother's pension.

This is an extreme but unfortunately increasingly common case. OK, my dad wasn't a great explainer and both my parents were really tough on me, but I got to see that there were reasons for some of the restrictions. They did instil in me basic values of discipline and hard work and the story of the girl at school highlights what can happen when you don't have any. Not that I'm pretending to have been a model child, of course! As it was my parents often thought my behaviour was terrible, but if they'd known what I really got up to sometimes, they would've locked me in my bedroom and never let me out! But the logic behind some of their strictness rubbed off on me and just before I would go too far I would stop myself. I would rather have been brought up the way I was than had the supposed 'dream' home life that my school mate had. My friends and I were all jealous of her but ultimately her lifestyle did her no good at all.

An important part of being a Teen Witch is understanding that the Craft is a discipline, and you're not going to get anywhere in magick without a lot in the way of self-control.

Probably only one or two of my friends had a family life that was really happy, where parents and children all got along and there was lots of love to share around. Unfortunately it's almost mandatory that a lot of the time teens and parents do not mix. It's part of life's journey, and the challenges of your teens can teach you to be strong and know yourself. I like who I am now and I am that person because of everything I've been through, and that includes the way I was brought up.

A challenging home life means that you have something to learn from. Often the most special people have had the hardest lessons, and you can use a difficult home life and the ups and downs of getting along with your parents as fuel to become a better person and a more powerful Teen Witch.

I wasn't a Teen Witch so I didn't make my home environment work for me. I was expelled from my school at fourteen, put into a special school for 'gifted but troubled' children at fifteen, which I left before I finished Year 10 because I got a job as model/receptionist for a clothing company. Mum and Dad didn't try to stop me – in fact, I think they were relieved to see me go! Things were really horrible at home and it was starting to badly affect my younger brother and sister. We had reached a dead end. Looking back I know that if I'd been practising Witchcraft I would have had a better appreciation of myself and have been less inclined to prove myself by rebelling and doing risky things that, although at the time seemed thrilling and fun, were ultimately not doing anyone any favours, least of all me.

Teen Witches know that, no matter what their parents say, no matter what the toughies at school say, they are special, sacred and an essential part of the Universe. Through their rituals and spells they can always be in touch with their inner magick and no-one can take this away from them.

Of course, this sense of personal power can also be used to create positive changes, rather than simply making the hard times less uncomfortable. There are spells you can do to bring more harmony into your relationship with your parents and spells you can do to make you a better person, more loving and appreciative of your parents and more at ease in your own skin.

When you have this understanding, home problems don't tend to bother you as much. If your parents do or say something that you think is unfair, you're more able to let it go rather than taking it on board and feeling that you have to defend yourself. You may even end up agreeing with them and realising that they are right! And, funnily enough, the more this happens the less your parents will give you grief and you may actually start to get along. There will always be problems, of course – they're a fact of life no matter how old you are – but challenges and obstacles are there to make our lives ultimately richer and more rewarding.

Before we get onto spells to help a difficult home life I want to remind you that attempting to change your parents' opinions or behaviour through spells is an extremely bad idea and they will certainly either fail to work or backfire horribly. Remember one of the Witches' Laws is: 'Do what you will, but do not interfere with another's free will.' Trying to manipulate anyone is disrespectful no matter how good you think your intentions are. As far as your parents go, using spells to try to force them to change makes the chances of you ever having a good relationship with them extremely remote. Manipulative magick is self-destructive at the best of times but becomes more so when directed at those we're closest to.

Having said that, the spells I give here are completely non-manipulative and work towards change in yourself and to increase your sense of balance in the world.

SORTING OUT YOUR SIBLINGS

When your sisters and/or brothers are sending you around the twist, you can use the spells suggested here to harmonise your relationship with them too. Just substitute their name/s and instead of saying 'parents' say 'siblings' or 'sister/brother'.

THE FORGIVE AND FORGET SPELL

This is a spell for when you have really hit a brick wall with your parents and no-one can open their mouths without saying something nasty. You are totally hurt and *over* it and they are fed up with you. Remember that in a situation like this neither you nor your parents are empowered – it's likely you are all just playing out a game of pre-programmed reactions. The person who really has their personal power together is the one who stops behaving like a Terminator and turns back into a human being. This spell is a way for you to do this.

However, it's a fairly demanding three-part spell, that will require a strong commitment of time and focus – but it works! It's also carried out over three phases of the moon: the waning moon, the waxing moon and the full moon. As you progress through the spell, you will notice things starting to improve, but the maximum positive impact will be felt around the full moon and onwards.

Part One

Best time: The waning moon
You will need:
* 1 black candle
* 1 black piece of paper
* 1 black pen
* 1 bulb of garlic
* 1 block of ice
* 1 knife
* 1 stick of patchouli incense, or a charcoal disc and leaves of patchouli crushed to a powder

Cast Circle, using the full ritual or snapping in an Instant Circle, lighting the incense as a part of this. Sit and meditate on the problems that you are experiencing with your parents. Go over individual arguments in your mind and dwell on hurtful things that were said. When you are ready, carve your first name and your parents' first names into the black candle with your knife, then lick your thumb and trace it over the names to seal them. Now light the candle, take a deep breath and intone:

> Flame of night
> Burning bright,
> Illuminate within me
> A spark of light.
> Power of fire,
> Lift me higher,
> Purge from me
> My darkest hour.

Now pick up the black pen, and on the black paper write out all the sadness and anger inside you. It may come as sentences, it may come as words, it may come as pictures.

Write on both sides of the paper and, if necessary, write on top of other writing. When the paper is coated with your feelings pick up the bulb of garlic and slice the top off it with your knife.

Hold the garlic in the hand that you write with and trace a big 'X' on both sides of the paper from the top to the bottom. As you do this say:

> I release pain and woe,
> From within me sadness flows.
> I am ready to forgive and forget,
> New ways of being come for the best.

Now light the patchouli incense and into your Circle invoke the ancient Greek Goddess and Patroness of Witches, Hecate, by saying:

> Hecate, Goddess of Old,
> May you bless me with your presence threefold.

Feel the powerful and magickally transformative energy of Hecate manifest herself in your Circle. When you feel her presence, wrap the paper around the block of ice and say:

> Hecate in your dark night,
> Freeze these words so that I might
> Be free to think well and good,
> New ways of being are understood.

Now say your Spell Sealing Charm:

> This I ask for the good of all
> So that harm may come to none,
> So Mote It Be,
> My will be done.

Now thank and farewell Hecate, close your Circle and bury the paper and the garlic under a tree, thanking it for its help in sealing your spell.

Part Two

Best time: The waxing moon
You will need:

- ✳ 1 light blue candle
- ✳ a blue ribbon
- ✳ a stick of lavender incense (or burn lavender on a charcoal disc)
- ✳ a picture of you and your parents together
- ✳ half a cup of crushed almonds
- ✳ a knife

Cast Circle, either in the full ritual or the Instant, and light the incense as a part of this. Carve your first name and your parents' first names into the candle with your knife, and again seal them by licking your thumb and tracing over the names.

Light the candle and sprinkle the crushed almonds around it in a circle. As you do this invoke the Goddess of the waxing moon, Artemis.

> *Artemis, bless me with your presence*
> *As you float in starry heavens,*
> *May our love grow strong and good*
> *As you grow waxing to full.*

Feel the silvery maiden, Artemis, and her blossoming, loving energy fill your Circle. Hold the photo in your hands, picturing your parents and yourself laughing together and enjoying wonderful happy times. When this is clear and strong in your mind, wrap the blue ribbon around the photo three times and tie five knots as you say the following:

By one, my will is done.
By two, it will come true.
By three, So Mote It Be.
By four, for the good of all.
By five, so shall love thrive.

Thank Artemis for her blessing and close the Circle. Keep
the photo and the candle in your bedroom and every night
leading up to the full moon, light it for a while and hold
the photo in both your hands as you gaze into the candle,
picturing you and your parents getting along brilliantly,
having great conversations and sharing lots of love.

Part Three

Best time: The full moon
You will need:

* ✳ 1 white or silver candle
* ✳ 1 stick of jasmine incense
* ✳ 1 white flower, perhaps a gardenia or a rose
* ✳ silver ribbon
* ✳ 1 piece of rose quartz crystal
* ✳ 1 white velvet cloth bag or white cardboard box
* ✳ sea salt
* ✳ a knife

Cast Circle, either in the full ritual or the Instant, and
lighting the incense as a part of this. Again, carve your first
name and your parents' first names into the candle and
seal them by licking your thumb and tracing over the
names.

Light the candle and sprinkle the sea salt in a circle
around it. Hold the flower and the crystal in your hands
and invoke the Goddess of the Full Moon, Selene:

> *Queen of the Sky, Great Mother, Selene,*
> *I ask you to bless my parents and me*
> *That we may live in harmony*
> *Growing together happily.*

As you feel Selene's wise and intensely loving presence fill your Circle, place the flower, crystal and photo with the blue ribbon in the bag or box. Wrap the silver ribbon around it and tie seven knots as you say:

> *One is love.*
> *Two is truth.*
> *Three is sacred.*
> *Four is balance.*
> *Five is power.*
> *Six is passion.*
> *Seven is strength.*

Now you have a magickal amulet that will continue your spell-working so that your relationship with your parents gets better and better. It will also work to help you move through and learn from the challenges that will naturally present themselves, rather than getting caught up in destructive and unproductive patterns.

To finish the Forgive and Forget spell, hold your amulet and say your Spell Sealing Charm:

> *This I ask for the good of all*
> *So that harm may come to none,*
> *So Mote It Be,*
> *My will be done.*

Thank Selene and close your Circle. Keep your amulet either on your altar or somewhere safe. You can charge it up whenever you need to by lighting the silver candle and again asking for Selene's blessing as you did above.

THE SPREADING LOVE RITUAL

This is one of the simplest things you can do. It may sound obvious, but the more love you give out, the more you will receive back. So do something unexpected and nice for your parents. Don't wait for their birthdays or Christmas celebrations – buy or make them a present. Give them a card in which you've written a poem about how much you appreciate them and all they've given you. Surprise them by cleaning the whole house when they are out one day. Just remember, the more Spreading Love rituals you do, the more love will come to you.

THE QUICK AND EASY PERFECT PARENTS SPELL

Best time: Anytime!
You will need:
* a white candle (for spirit and the element of fire)
* a stick of strawberry incense (for fun and the element of air)
* a bowl of salt (for purity and the element of earth)
* a bowl of spring water (for emotions and the element of water)

Snap in an Instant Circle and light the candle and incense.
Look at all your goodies and let the heady scent of strawberry fill your heart with joy. Now say firmly:

> *I respect and love my parents;*
> *They respect and love me;*
> *We can live and learn joyfully.*

Hold the candle and say:

> *Fire, speed my wish to me.*

Hold the incense and say:

> *Air, bring me new energy.*

Hold the salt and say:

> *Earth, make me strong.*

Hold the water and say:

> *Water, fill me with love.*

Close Circle – the spell is done!

POWERFUL AFFIRMATIONS

This affirmation is great for when you are in the middle of an
argument with your parents and you want it to stop. To do
this, you have to stop fuelling it. Say to yourself:

> *I let go of anger, I let go of sadness. I am perfect and*
> *sacred. I can stop this madness.*

Except for a few extreme cases most parents do deserve
their children's respect. The job of a parent is surely the
most difficult and underrated on the planet. It's important
that as a Teen Witch you respect your elders as well-
intentioned human beings, regardless of whether you agree
with everything they say and every choice they make.
Because the bottom line is most of the time they are doing
the best they can at a very demanding job. As you get older
you'll find this out – especially if you become a parent
yourself.

An excellent affirmation for appreciating and getting along with your parents is very simple. Say:

Goddess, help me to understand, love and respect my parents.

She will.

School Sux!

Out of all the requests for spells and rituals I get from Teen Witches via my website, it's always school and love which come across as the most pressing issues. And why not, since you spend most of your teenage life there? In this chapter I have put together lots of spells which hopefully will provide you with the tools you need to get the most out of these important years.

Note: Don't forget to check out the magickal properties of the herbs, crystals, colours etc. that you are using in the 'Magickal Meanings' chapter.

BORING CLASS SPELL

Here is a spell to do for the class that makes you fall asleep
– whether it's the subject or the teacher, the boredom is
killing you!

Best time: When you need it!

You will need:

* A yellow candle
* A teaspoon of celery seed
* Lemon essential oil
* A yellow piece of paper
* Lemon juice
* A feather to use as a writing quill
* A sealable envelope or small bag

At home, light the yellow candle and by this light dip your
feather quill into the lemon juice, writing the following
on the piece of paper (you don't need to see the words,
just trace their intent onto the paper – but keep dipping
the quill into the juice to harness the clarifying energy of
the lemon):

> *I (name) do declare*
> *The powers of mind*
> *Are strong and clear;*
> *Fascinating is my course*
> *I enjoy with magick force.*

Now fold the paper over until it is a small triangle and drip
three drops of the lemon oil on it. Place this and the celery
seeds into the envelope or bag and seal. Hold the charm
between both hands and gaze at the candle flame as you
repeat the incantation three more times.

Take the charm with you to class and, when you
feel you are drifting off, shake the charm so that the seeds
rattle and say the invocation to restate the spell. You will

immediately feel clearer and more able to enjoy the class. Keep charging up this spell by rattling the seeds as often as necessary.

HORRIBLE TEACHER SPELL

Teachers are only human, and capable of making mistakes, but when I was at school I used to put them on a pedestal and was either worshipping them, terrified of them or hating them. Teaching is one of the most demanding and yet undervalued jobs in Western society (along with motherhood) so it's important that you respect your teachers and acknowledge they are most likely doing the best they can in an often difficult and frustrating system. So if sometimes they are brilliant and inspiring and at others just plain awful, be tolerant. But if you find yourself lumbered with a teacher who seems to enjoy torturing students, here's a spell to help sort them out. Note, though, that this isn't a curse or anything totally, hideously, viciously nasty. (Oh, c'mon, don't go sulky on me.)

Best time: It can give extra oomph! to do this spell on a Saturday during the waning moon, but any time is appropriate.

You will need:
* A black candle
* A white candle
* 4 senna pods (or half a teaspoon of the powder)
* Some soil scooped from the imprint of the teacher's footprint (you may have to be ingenious to get this. Make sure they don't see you do it!)
* A small pot plant of heart's ease (a type of violet)

* A sharp pin
* A piece of black paper
* A black pen
* A small jug of spring water

Carve your teacher's name with a pin on the black candle, and then on the piece of paper write down all the horrible things they do and say, covering both sides of the paper if necessary. Now stand the black candle on the paper, light it and say:

> *On this paper, dark and forlorn,*
> *The written words are hurting.*
> *I bind these so they have no form,*
> *Now letters with no meaning.*

Fold the paper over once and drip a drop of wax on it, then fold it again, dripping one drop of wax each time until the paper is folded into a small square. Now burn the paper in the flame of the black candle, being careful to keep the ashes.

Carve the teacher's name into the white candle and light it. Focus on the healing and renewing energies of the pure white candle and its fire.

When you are ready, mix the ash from the paper in with the soil from your teacher's footprint and sprinkle in a sunwise (anti-clockwise) direction around the pot plant. Then press the four senna pods into the base of the pot plant (or sprinkle the powder around the base).

Now slowly pour the water over the soil as you say:

> *Nourishing the energies of love and compassion,*
> *So grows this plant with healthy abandon.*
> *Blessed and honoured is this new situation,*
> *Free from the past, new patterns created.*

Now say the Spell Sealing charm:

> *This I ask for the good of all*
> *So that harm may come to none,*
> *So Mote it Be,*
> *My will be done.*

Keep looking after the little plant and watch your relationship with your teacher improve!

Note: this spell can be adapted to include other people with whom you have a poor relationship – you are not seeking to change their behaviour beyond their free will, you are just banishing sadness and hurt and encouraging new, more loving and compassionate energies to blossom.

LEAVE MY THINGS ALONE SPELL!

I remember the first time something was stolen from me at school – I was devastated! My parents had just taken us kids on a holiday to Tasmania. I was twelve and I had a fantastic time, the highlight being our visit to an enormous lavender farm. (I must have been Witchy even before I was consciously aware of it – I was fascinated by the herb and its uses. Maybe that's why it's one of my faves to this day!)

In addition to dried lavender, lavender oil and lavender jam, I also brought home a strange souvenir. It was a dried apple fashioned into the head of a little old wise woman wearing a white cap, white kitchen apron and chequered skirt. She was carrying a little straw broom and was very Witchy!

I kept her in my desk at school and every chance I got I would open the desk and look at her. I felt I had a special friend hiding away in there (especially as I didn't have any friends outside my desk). I usually remembered to put her away in my locker if one of my classes wasn't in my home room, but one day I didn't. When I returned she was gone. I remember being really shocked that someone would take something that wasn't theirs. This may sound naïve, but at the time it really freaked me out and took quite a while to get over!

So here is a little ritual that you can do to help protect your belongings from interference by another. Of course, you have to take appropriate action on the physical plane – don't be careless or leave things lying around that you don't want others to fiddle with – but this ritual will help assure your belongings' safety.

With your power finger or your athame, trace a pentagram surrounded by a circle (with the points of the star touching it) over the object or area you want protected. In your mind's eye see the pentagram form as electric blue light. Now all you need to do is empower the protective shield by directing the palm of your power hand towards the object. Feel the palm of your hand heat up as you channel your energy and desire into the pentagram shield, which you should see glow and pulse in your mind's eye.

The object is now protected. You can create this shield over just about anything, not just objects but doorways to discourage unwanted people entering, or even whole buildings. When I was writing this book in a very beautiful but remote country house, on the nights I was alone I would trace a giant blue circled pentagram over the roof of the house with my mind's eye to protect me as I slept.

Note: Don't physically touch the object. I know some Witches who trace pentagrams into the dusty bonnets of their cars to protect them – but it's really better to do it in your mind's eye, even if it's just to avoid arousing the interest of anyone who doesn't understand the sacred meaning of the five-pointed star. Unfortunately the symbol has been debased as a Satanic and negative symbol for some time (though gradually this is changing) and you don't want any hassles – you want your stuff left alone!

QUICK HELP FOR STUDYING AND EXAMS

You will need:
* A piece of citrine quartz
* A piece of clear quartz
* Rosemary oil
* An oil burner

Before you study for an exam, burn five drops of rosemary oil in water on the oil burner. Hold the citrine in your right hand and the clear quartz in your left, inhale the scent of rosemary and say: 'My mind is clear, my knowledge good – success is mine' and start studying.

Before your exam place a drop of rosemary oil on your temples and place the crystals on the desk while you do your exam.

A SPELL FOR MENTAL STRENGTH TO HELP DEAL WITH SCHOOL BULLIES

I got picked on heaps at school. I don't know why – I tried to fit in – but whether it was older girls pushing me down stairs or my so-called friends one day just deciding to ignore me for a week, there was always something wrong. The following spell helps give you strength to deal with those peers who make your life a misery. Their poor behaviour will be like water off a duck's back to you and eventually they will give up and leave you alone.

You will need:

* A handful of borage blossoms or leaves
* Dragon's blood powder
* Sandalwood powder
* A piece of tiger's eye (which is a crystal)
* A yellow silk pouch
* A red candle
* A drop of your blood (or from the person needing the spell!)

To a handful of borage blossoms or leaves, add a teaspoon of dragon's blood powder and a teaspoon of sandalwood powder. Grind these together and add a piece of tiger's eye and a drop of blood from the person needing the spell.

Place all this in the yellow silk pouch and light the red candle. Holding the pouch in both hands, call on the Archangel Michael (note you pronounce it Mee-kay-el. If you pronounce it the regular way, you might end up with Mikey Robins or someone manifesting!):

Archangel Michael, avail me of the power of your mighty sword to cut down my oppressors and free me to be whole.

Carry the pouch at all times to ward off problems and recharge its powers by lighting the red candle and calling on the Archangel.

Another spell, and one of my favourites, which can help freeze the actions of people picking on you or giving you grief is:

THE FREEZE OFF! SPELL

Write the name or names of the people that you want to bind from tormenting you on a tiny piece of black paper and put it in an ice cube tray with a clove of garlic with an 'X' carved into it with a pin. Pour water over it and freeze. The creeps will leave you alone.

THE 'I'M NOT NERVOUS' AMULET

Whether it's the school play, the night before exams, or having to make important decisions about your future, keeping this amulet with you can enhance your personal vibrations and align you with fortuitous energies.

Best time: Sunday, to infuse with positive solar energy
You will need:

* A purple velvet or silk pouch or bag about the size of your palm
* A teaspoon of powdered sandalwood
* A piece of white agate crystal
* Six pinches of St John's Wort herb
* A gold candle
* Your favourite perfume or scent (one that makes you feel fabulous and focused when you wear it). If you don't have one, get one!

Lay all the things out, light the gold candle and spray three squirts of perfume over the flame (be careful as the alcohol in the perfume will flare up) as you say:

> I infuse these objects with my will,
> The power's mine to get my fill.
> Confidence and bravery come to be
> When this amulet is with me.

Now put all the objects into the amulet bag and spray with a squirt of perfume or scent. Hold the amulet pouch in both hands, gaze into the flame and concentrate strongly on being able to remember your lines, study for your test or make your decisions easily and effortlessly. Say the charm one more time and snuff the candle – the spell is done. You can recharge the amulet anytime by holding it and repeating the charm.

THE 'I AM LOSING THE PLOT' SPELL

Sometimes the pressure of exams or homework can just do your head in and you start losing the plot. The following spell is one of healing and re-empowerment which will help you get back on track and coping again.

You will need:
 * A silver candle
 * A blue candle
 * Three drops of cinnamon oil (for boys) or neroli (for girls)
 * Six drops of rose geranium (calming, healing and loving)
 * A sharp pin

With the pin, carve your name into both candles and anoint with the blended oils. Light both candles, and as they burn imagine streams of silver and blue light swirling together around and above the candle flames. Picture yourself feeling calm and well, at peace with your place in the world. Then call on the Witches' Goddess:

> Lady of Light, I now call forth
> For I need your strength and form,
> Light my steps, clear my head,
> So I tread the path for which I'm meant.

Keep focusing on the swirling blue light and then see in your mind's eye an image of yourself with that light swirling around you, healing and strengthening. When you are ready, snuff the candles and repeat this spell at least once a day until the situation improves.

YOU'RE ON A WITCH HUNT

Here's a spell to deal with schoolmates, teachers – anyone who is ridiculing you or hassling you for being a Witch. Of course, you can always do the 'Freeze Off' spell to get them to leave you alone, but this one can work more specifically not only to stop them bothering you but also to help heal them from their prejudice and lack of compassion.

Best time: On Friday (ruled by Venus, planet of unconditional love) during the waxing moon.

You will need:

* A black candle
* A pink candle
* Rose geranium oil
* A dill seed
* Nine cloves
* Three large pins with red or white heads on them

Cast Circle. Carve the names of the person/people whom you want to accept your choices without judgement into the black candle – if there are too many or you don't know their names carve a line for each one. Lick your thumb and trace over the carvings with your spit to bind your energy to theirs for a short time.

Place the candle in a stand and, around it, place the nine cloves in an even circle. Light the candle and hold your hands over the warmth of the candle flame, channelling your energy into the candle (be careful when you do this – once when I did it the candle flame leapt up really high and strong and burnt my palm!).

As you project your energy, slowly say this incantation:

I reverse all that is adverse,
Bound to me, no longer cursed;

> *Ill feelings gone, the tide is turned,*
> *I am free, no longer spurned.*

Now with your left hand (or the hand you don't write with) gather the cloves up in a widdershins (clockwise or against the sun) direction to release your binding to these people. Put the candle and the cloves to one side to be buried later.

Now anoint the pink candle with a few drops of rose geranium oil, rubbing in well. Sprinkle the dill seeds around the base in a deosil (sunwise, anti-clockwise) direction. Light the candle and sit and meditate for a moment on the qualities of compassion and love. Think about how really powerful people don't hold grudges or resent others for their lack of knowledge or lack of understanding but instead seek to heal unpleasant and imbalanced situations with love.

When you are ready, take one of the pins and hold it in the flame of the candle until the metal is hot. Then push the pin through the 'heart area' of the candle (about three-quarters of the way up) as you say:

> *Here I declare Love to feel, Love to share.*

Do the same with the second pin, pressing it into the candle at the 'throat area' (a bit higher up) and say:

> *Here I declare Words are kind, Words are fair.*

Do the same with the third pin, pressing it into the 'third eye area' (higher up again) and say:

> *Here I declare Thoughts that care.*

Now hold your hands over the flame and project your energy as you say:

> *Let no person, thing or time*
> *Undo the charm I set to rhyme.*

Then, for extra oomph!, you could add the spell-sealing charm:

This I ask for the good of all,
So that harm may come to none,
So Mote it Be,
My will be done.

Now, if you like, you can leave the candle burning, or snuff the flame and keep the candle and dill seeds wrapped in white cloth and hidden in a drawer somewhere for at least another three full moons to keep the spell charged.

After closing Circle, bury the black candle and cloves in some dirt. After three full moons you can bury the pink candle and dill seeds. If the problem persists do the spell in full again.

PENCIL SHAVINGS SPELL

This one is really easy – you can even do it in class! It's great for releasing blocked energy, dispersing unpleasant situations or keeping heated situations under control.

You will need:
* 1 lead pencil
* 1 sharpener

On a white piece of paper, write down the problem with the pencil, for example: 'the student behind me keeps bugging me to tell her the answers to the test'. Next, take the sharpener and sharpen the pencil three full turns, letting the shavings fall on the paper, then fold the paper and repeat the process. By now the student should have stopped doing it. Or, if, for example, there is tension between you and another class mate or your teacher, you could write: 'energy is blocked – the situation stopped'. Keep writing, sharpening and folding to keep the situation from blowing up further. Just throw the paper and shavings in the bin when you're done (or in the incinerator if you don't want people to read what you've written!).

ERASER SPELL

This is another easy one to do in class. It's great if you're having trouble learning something.

You will need:
- ✳ 1 lead pencil or pen
- ✳ 1 eraser or white-out liquid

Write the problem on a piece of white paper, for example: 'I cannot understand this maths equation'. Look at what you've written and be aware of the emotions inside you as you contemplate your problem. You may become aware that you have always been told by your father, 'you'll never succeed at anything because you never stick at anything long enough' (that's what I was always told!). Or you may become aware of a deep feeling of pressure because you are so scared of getting something wrong that you'd rather not try it in the first place. Try to isolate the real problem – it's probably not the difficulty of the maths equation or how smart you are: its more likely your feelings about your capabilities. When you are confident you have isolated the emotion or thought, channel it into your hand, pick up the eraser or white-out liquid and 'rub out' that emotion by erasing your written sentence. When it is gone, know that you have removed the problem and get on with solving that equation!

ANOTHER STUDY SPELL

This is another good one to help with studying – it helps create a conducive environment for absorbing knowledge. This spell involves making 'Merlyn's Powder of Knowledge'.

You will need:
* 1 purple candle
* frankincense or lavender incense
* Merlyn's Powder of Knowledge:
    * 3 teaspoons powdered nutmeg
    * 2 teaspoons of crushed patchouli leaves (if you can't get these, double up on the lavender)
    * 1 teaspoon of black pepper
    * 1 teaspoon of crushed lavender
    * 2 teaspoons of corn flour
    * some filings from your nails. Use a nail file and capture them on paper – if you bite your fingernails, use your toenails (and do the self love spell on page xx later so that you stop eating yourself up!).

Mix all the above either with your hands in a glass or china bowl or in a mortar and pestle (this is best).

Cast Circle, lighting the purple candle and incense as

part of your Circle casting. Call on the Magickal Master
of Learning, Knowledge and Wisdom, Merlyn:

I invoke thee Merlyn,
Master of Learning;
Avail me of your Ability
To know and learn easily.

Merlyn's presence will feel solid and comforting, but also
tingly and intellectually stimulating. Merlyn makes learning fun and exciting no matter what the subject! Feel
imbued with his power: everything is magickal and possible and you will become aware that all the knowledge you
absorb will be put to profound and good use.

Now that you are charged up, pick up the Knowledge
Powder and hold it towards the candle flame, saying:

I charge this Powder with Learning Powers
As Merlyn decrees my Knowledge flowers.

Focus on the Powder absorbing Merlyn's essence – the ingredients will be receptive to this energy and absorb it well.

When you are ready say 'It is done' and close Circle in
the usual way, thanking Merlyn for his assistance.

You can use the powder by sprinkling a little around
where you are studying, whether it's on the floor or around
your books or computer. If you are worried about making
a mess, sprinkle some around the base of the purple candle
and have that burning as you study. Or have a small bowl
with some of the powder in it. You could also place a citrine
or clear quartz in your study area and sprinkle a little
around that. You can also put some of the powder into a
little cloth bag (purple is a good colour) and carry it with
you – if you do this pop a piece of the quartz in with it.
For an extra hit of knowledge power, throw some of the
powder onto a lit charcoal disc as incense.

COLOUR SPELL

This is another really simple one!

Check the colour correspondences in 'Magickal Meanings' for colours that correspond to your goals and needs. For example, you would like more pocket money so you can afford to buy a new outfit to look great, so choose green for money, yellow for intellect (to help you make the best choice) and pink for self-love.

On white paper, draw a pentagram with each colour over the top of each other, focusing on your desire. Kiss the magick sigil (a sigil is a sign or symbol with magickal power) three times and fold the paper into a small square. Every day for seven days, open the paper, stare at the sigil focusing intently on your wish before kissing it three times and folding it up again. Do this morning and night and within the week your wish will start to manifest.

QUICK CALMING SPELL

This one's great for when you're feeling nervous: before an exam, before an interview with the headmistress, or even before getting off the school bus because the boy or girl you like is there.

You will need:
* A piece of amethyst crystal
* A handful of chamomile
* A teaspoon of sandalwood powder
* A blue mojo bag

Mix the chamomile and sandalwood together with your power hand as you say this incantation:

Powers of sacred herb and sacred wood,
Calm my nerves so all is good;

Restore a sense of peace to me,
So I conquer fear and am at peace.

Place the mixture in the bag and place in it the amethyst crystal. The amethyst will amplify the soothing and restorative energies of the herb and wood so that your energies align with their peaceful presence, your mind will be clear and you will be capable of your duties. Keep the bag in your pocket and give it a squish with your hand when you need to churn up its powers.

Another good tip for keeping your cool is to wear a sandalwood bead necklace or bracelet (try Indian import stores and new age stores). Sandalwood also helps making learning easy so wearing it at school is a good move.

Also upon awakening on a potentially stressful day place slices of cucumber on your eyelids for five minutes and in your mind's eye picture a vast calm ocean. This will also soothe you (and take any puffiness from a restless sleep away from your eyes!). Cucumber can open up the powers of the subconscious and help you be more in touch with the big picture of your life.

Speaking of restless sleep, here's an excellent sleep tonic that will knock you out and give you a peaceful night's rest the night before that exam, sporting carnival or big date.

You will need:

* ¹/₂ a handful of hops
* a small handful of red clover (pick it fresh from your garden)
* ¹/₄ teaspoon of tarragon
* three pieces of lettuce (chopped)

Steep all the ingredients in a saucepan of almost boiling water for five minutes, then strain and drink – and go straight to bed!

If you have been having nightmares because you are stressed out over school, or anything really, place a piece of amethyst crystal under your pillow for good dreams and a restful sleep.

I'M A SQUARE PEG IN A ROUND HOLE SPELL

Peer pressure is the worst, except for perhaps having no pressure because no-one acknowledges you exist! I copped both extremes at school. One of my main memories of school is of finally having a group to hang out with but always being on the edge of the pack. Walking down the hill from the bus stop to school I was always on the perimeter of our group, leaning in, straining to hear what the 'coolest' girls were saying and trying to laugh and bitch at the appropriate times. The following spell puts you in touch with your inner power. At this point it's worth mentioning that all the things that are valued as cool at school are the least important attributes when you leave. So if you don't fit in, take it as a sign that you are capable of doing something really spectacular when you leave. Get everything you need out of school selfishly – don't let others distract you from your personal goals and power.

Best time: Sunday as the moon waxes (this time is important as you need to make the most of the prevailing solar and lunar energies).

You will need:
* 1 green candle
* 1 pink candle
* 1 small magnet
* 1 tablespoon sunflower oil

* ✳ 3 drops rosemary oil
* ✳ 2 drops lemon oil
* ✳ ¹/₂ teaspoon dragon's blood powder
* ✳ Nag champa incense (you can get it from just about every health food and new age/Witchy supply store – it's a wonderfully inspiring blend from India)
* ✳ One hair from your head

Burn the incense as you mix the oils together and stir through the dragon's blood powder. Place in a small bottle and pop the magnet in.

Anoint the green and pink candles and light. Now anoint yourself – a dab on your third eye (between your eyebrows), over your heart and over your solar plexus (just below the rib cage) and get ready for maximum empowerment!

Inhale slowly and connect with your deep sense of self – the one that goes beyond other people's opinions of you, or even your immediate opinions of yourself. Deep inside there is a place Witches call 'the Green': it's the fertile and eternally renewing essence of your personal power. Sometimes its presence may only be perceived as the tiniest of sparks, at other times it may be an enormous, lush, glowing sphere. When you are connected hold your hands towards the candles and let the fuel of their sacred candle fire be drawn inside you to the Green stoking it up, so that your whole being feels strong, passionate and unique (it's your personal power). When you are ready, pick up the oil, holding it towards the candle flame and intone:

> *Sacred oil of Dragon Fire,*
> *potion of power heed my desire;*

> *By day and night fuel my might*
> *Growing stronger – ever bright.*

Feel the bottle of oil grow hot in your hands as energy pours into it. Now place your hair in the bottle, binding your physical and spiritual essence to its contents.

When you are ready, snuff the candles and keep the bottle safe – somewhere private. No-one must use this oil except you. Every morning dab a little on the soles of your feet so that you always take empowered steps. This oil is not only for empowerment but also attraction and you will find as you use it that people will genuinely start to seek out your company because they will sense your new strength and be drawn to it.

LEAVING SCHOOL SPELL

OK, you've decided to leave school. Whether you're about to enter university, start a job or go backpacking around Europe so that you can have a break, this spell seals the school experience, helping you to consolidate your time there, release it and move onto the rest of your life. It's good to do this spell the morning after your final school day.

Best time: just before dawn

You will need:
*   A handful of dried rue
*   A handful of dried sage
*   Small branches of willow (fallen from the tree and dried) for a small fire
*   1 teaspoon of sandalwood powder
*   1 dark blue candle
*   1 pale blue candle
*   paper (to help start the fire)

Mix the sage, rue and sandalwood together in a bowl.

Make a small (safe!) fire with the willow and paper and set the blue candles up either side. Light the fire and wait for the sun to rise. As the sun rises throw one half of the herb mix into the fire as you say:

> *Sacred herbs and fire light,*
> *rising sun new and bright,*
> *bless my efforts of the past,*
> *launch me on my future path.*

Sit quietly and meditate on your time at school – don't judge anything as good or bad – just let memories flow through your mind like water. When you are ready throw the second half of the herb mix into the fire and say the incantation again. This time, meditate on your plans for the future. Again, don't judge, just let your ideas flow throw your mind.

When the fire has burnt down, collect some of the ash and place it in a container. You can use this ash for future spells requiring extra strength or transformative powers as it has absorbed your presence and the essence of your efforts from your school years. Just add a pinch to any incense blend or herb mixture.

Snuff the blue candles and get on with the rest of your life!

Doing What You Will

Unfortunately, some Teen Witches have to keep their spiritual path a secret because their parents, friends or teachers don't understand or tolerate their interests. For this reason, I've written a special chapter for those who are on the Path, but have to put up with people trying to push them off!

You may have tried to help them understand that you do not do evil things, that you do not worship Satan – all the worst misconceptions about the Craft – but they will not listen. If you do need to express your Witchcraft secretly, it's not about being sneaky and lying, both of which practices will inhibit your personal magickal development: it's about being resourceful and inventive so that you don't have to abandon your Craft until a time when you are able to express yourself freely.

In this book I've addressed ways of exploring the Craft if your parents, teachers and/or friends are not very accepting or even approving of your interests. As a young person it's a brave and wise thing to make a choice to willingly explore a spiritual path – especially Witchcraft . . . because it's the best! Oh, OK, I'm prejudiced, I know! Whether it's the 'best' for you or not (only you can decide that), one thing is certain: the Craft is one of the most widely misunderstood of all the Western world's religions. So here, in a nutshell, are a few tips on 'doing what you will'.

First and foremost: how do you tell your parents and friends that you are a Witch? Well, before rushing into this, ask yourself whether it's really necessary to do it at all. I didn't let anyone know about my growing interest in the Craft for quite a few years – I just read about it, explored it, tried things out in private until I felt confident in 'coming out of the broom closet'. (That phrase, by the way, makes a strong statement about this whole issue: being drawn to the Craft can raise exactly the same sort of issues as being gay can. While more and more people in our society are cool about both subjects, coming out as Wiccan or gay can still be difficult, depending on how your family and friends feel about the subject. Also, different people will feel differently about just how 'out' they want to be, and it's completely right for them to make up their own minds.) However, if you do want to tell them, or if your Mum found some Witchy things in your room and asked you, 'What the hell is all this?', what can you say?

First, reassure them that, despite what they may have heard, Witchcraft (in particular, Wicca) has nothing to do with Satanism or hurting people, animals or yourself. Let them know that as a Teen Witch you find nature sacred, you acknowledge not only a God but also a Goddess, and you do rituals to honour these. You also do spells to help and heal and to get the most out of your life. You could also tell your parents that there are three laws that, as a Witch, you must abide by:

1. Do what you want to do as long as you don't hurt anyone.
2. Do what you want to do as long as you don't interfere with another's free will.
3. That which you send out returns upon you, three-fold – minimum!

When or if you talk to your parents about Witchcraft it's important that you emphasise you're interest in Wicca because you love being alive, you want to make the most out of your life, and to be the very best you can be: which is what Witchcraft is all about.

If they won't listen or don't understand, or are worried or ridiculing you, stop referring to your Craft as Witchcraft and call it Wicca instead: you may find that not saying such a provocative word will provide breathing space while they get used to the idea.

Remember, the way to address fear and ignorance is with love and knowledge. No-one is perfect, adults included, and sometimes things that are different freak people out and they react by judging and rejecting those things. Just be patient and remember as a Teen Witch you don't have to prove anything to anyone: the Path you follow is the one you forge yourself.

THE CLAYTONS ALTAR

Possibly some of you may be too young to remember an advertisement for a non-alcoholic drink called 'Claytons'. It was promoted for adults as 'the drink you have when you're not having a drink' – so you can have an altar – without having an altar.

Your parents may forbid you to have an altar in your room, or they might even destroy one you have set up. This can be very distressing – I remember my father breaking my vinyl records when I accidentally played one too loud because I didn't realise he was in the house. No questions were asked; he just came in, tore the record off the stereo and broke it and the few others I was allowed to own. That really upset me, and I can't even begin to think how I would have felt if I'd had an altar in my room and he'd smashed that.

You can have a Teen Witch's altar in your room that doesn't attract attention and doesn't look obviously Witchy. You only need to have the elements represented and something for the Lady and Lord. For example, you could have a feather for air, a crystal or stone for earth, an unlit candle for fire, and a vase with water (for water) and fresh flowers for the Lady and leafy branches for the Lord (of the Forests).

Or you could have a photo altar, setting up photos in

frames or even sticking them on the wall. Water could be a picture of the ocean, a volcano or sun can be fire, the sky and clouds for air and a mountain for earth. And a photo of a special woman and man for the Lady and Lord (I have some beautiful esoteric cards featuring amazing looking men and women to reinforce the presence of the Lady and Lord at my altar).

What about toys? Even stuffed ones! A bird for air, a cow for earth (cows and bulls were some of the first animals to work with humans helping to till soil as we developed our agricultural skills), a bee or cat for fire (the golden colour of honey represents the sun and the Egyptian Sun Goddess, Bast, is often represented as a cat) and a fish for water.

When you understand what the symbolism and roles of the traditional altar pieces are, then you are only limited by your imagination as to how you make your own 'Claytons' altar meaningful and potent.

Part of being a Teen Witch is being just that: a Teen. So don't feel you have to do things exactly like adult Witches. While you are living with your parents or guardians, you have to respect the fact that you live under their roof and it is appropriate and honourable for you to respect their rules and expectations. You just need to be resourceful and use your intuition to get around certain obstacles (like them not respecting your interests).

I'M BURNING UP

As I have said before, candles and incense may pose a threat to your parents as they don't want the house burnt down: fair enough. When I was living at home I was forbidden to burn incense because my Dad thought the sweet smelling smoke was drugs! No matter how much I tried to tell him incense wasn't intoxicating, he wouldn't listen.

Teen Witches can use candles of every colour without lighting them. Until you are allowed to, visualise them burning by being aware of the qualities of heat and the powerful 'moving and shaking' energy that a flame conjures. You can power-up unlit candles by using a pin to carve your name (or the intent of a spell) and then rubbing a few drops of appropriate essential oil (the one suggested in the spell or ritual, or if none is suggested use lavender) over the carving as you visualise the element of fire.

You can also use a feather instead of incense to represent the element of air. Perhaps even place a few drops of essential oil (relevant to your spell or ritual) on a feather and wave that through the air, to enjoy the scent and invoke the mood and energies you normally would by lighting incense.

PUT THAT KNIFE DOWN!

An athame looks pretty formidable and pretty lethal to those who don't understand what it's for. It's *never* used for cutting anything solid. It *is* used for directing and focusing energy and for cutting portals in the etheric and astral planes (for example, in adept Witches' Circle casting rituals, the invoking and banishing pentagrams for each quarter are created when calling on the Guardians of the Elements).

Instead of an athame, you can use your power finger (the index finger of your right hand or, if you prefer, your left if this is the hand you write with). Or you can use your wand or even a feather. I sometimes don't use my athame and use my power finger instead, especially when I'm travelling a lot. (I got sick of having to explain that the twelve-inch knife in my hand luggage was a religious artifact every time I went through a metal detector at an airport!)

THE INVISIBLE BOOK OF SHADOWS

A lot of Teen Witches have told me that their parents, on finding their Book of Shadows, promptly burnt it. Maybe you could leave it in your locker at school, or keep it on a computer disc (though as I say in the section on Book of Shadows on page 66, handwritten and embellished hard copy is often more satisfying). Do a 'Leave Me Alone' charm to help keep it undisturbed. A Book of Shadows is an important part of a Teen Witch's knowledge and experience, documenting as it does this fertile time of your Witchy development – so don't leave it lying around. If you have to hide it, make sure it's in a good spot. (How about inside the trunk of a hollow tree? Wrapped in something waterproof and mouseproof, of course.)

FOR THE BOOKWITCH

Reading is always a big part of Witchy research and you might want to consider using libraries for your Witchy research rather than filling your shelves with books your folks might take exception to. Or maybe do most of your research using the Internet – although it is possible that your folks may keep an eye on what sites you've been to, material you've saved, and so on, so don't assume your computer is private space unless you know way more about computers than your parents!

CAN I PLEASE HAVE SOME PRIVACY?

Circles outdoors in a safe place are often even better than Circles in your room (especially if you're worried you'll be disturbed at home). However I must stress that the place needs to be very safe: certainly not in the middle of nowhere, unless you are with a group of older people who can handle any situation. Even protection spells are not entirely infallible so always be sensible and safe and tell someone you trust where you are going.

AND FINALLY . . .

You don't need to go around advertising that you are a Witch and making a big visible statement about it all the time. Being a Witch is not about rebelling against your parents, or about what you wear, or bragging, or having power over other people. It is about tapping into the power inside you; it's about being the best you can be; it's about love and getting what you want out of life. So be proud of your choices and, don't take any criticism personally. Don't feel you have to be on a crusade all the time to make people understand you – just be true to yourself and your goals, and use your Witchcraft to help you achieve them.

Teen Witch in Love

PUCKER UP!

From when I was thirteen I was obsessed with boys, and often to my detriment! I went from being an A-grade student to a D-grade student in a term – seriously! I guess it was normal enough, but I lost all sense of myself and thought that the best I could be was based on whether some boy liked me. The girls in the group I hung out with were a bit older than me and were sort of tough and, to me, seemed to have their act together a lot more than I did. Their boyfriends were older and cooler but I got stuck with guys that were just as nervous as me. My friends set me up with this guy who, when I sat down next to him at the bus stop, jumped three inches off the seat! We didn't last very long!

The next guy I 'went out with', Sam, was a bit more confident, but one day two of my girlfriends and I jigged school to go and see the movie *Saturday Night Fever* which had just come out (I'm showing my age here!). My two friends sat behind Sam and me with their boyfriends. It was so humiliating: the whole way through the movie they kept issuing instructions like, 'OK, Sam, put your arm around Fiona', 'Give him a cuddle, Fiona, c'mon are you chicken?' By the end I was leaning so far out into the aisle that Sam's arm was nearly popping out of its socket as he attempted to keep it around me. When we were outside I tried to be cool and said 'Good movie, huh?' but Sam just walked away. The next day at school one of my girl-friends came up to me and said, 'Sam says to say, "You're dropped".'

For weeks after this I was increasingly pressured by the girls in my group since I was the only one who hadn't been kissed and they were starting to call me frigid! There was another boy, George, who had been acting keen for a while – he wasn't too bad, he had the bluest eyes I'd ever seen but his face was loaded with acne and, to be honest, I didn't want to get that close to it! But on my fourteenth birthday my day of reckoning had come. There was no escaping it. The girls had set it up that I would meet George by the side of the sewing cottage at my girls-only school and there the deed would be done. I was standing there, feeling so nervous that I was about to throw up (which probably wouldn't have made the whole thing any less romantic now I think of it), and then George sauntered along. He looked more cocky than he probably felt. My group was standing a short distance away eyeing us both off. George and I exchanged a few words: 'Hot isn't it?', 'Yeah'. Then, all off a sudden, my vision was blocked by his blurred face and – whack! – it landed on me. What 'it' was isn't easily described. It definitely didn't seem to have a lot in common with any screen kisses I'd seen at the movies. Perhaps I could best describe it as 'a slobbering chin chew'. He'd missed nearly all of both lips, which was quite an achievement at such close range, but he managed to catch a bit of the bottom one. On the good side, most of his tongue didn't get anywhere near the inside of my mouth. On the not so good side, it spent most of the interaction slobbering all over my chin.

I couldn't move or breathe, and then finally, after what seemed eternity, it was over. 'See ya this arvo at the bus stop' George said, and was gone. Yep, he was every bit as romantic with words as he was with his kisses. I slowly lifted my hand to my chin and wiped his spit away as the girls ran over. 'Why didn'tcha put ya arms 'round him?' they asked. I tried to tell them that he'd grabbed me so fast they'd stayed pinned against my chest where I'd had them crossed before the alleged magic moment, but I found I didn't really want to talk about it. I just felt sad that something I'd hoped would be so special turned out to be so disappointing. As kisses went it had been about as magical as being hit in the face with an over-ripe mango!

Since I wouldn't wish that sort of fiasco on anyone, and since some of you might have that first kiss experience in front of you, the following is a spell to help you prepare for that big event in your life. Whether you are nervous and want to wait, or eager and want to hurry up, this spell can work for you. It is primarily a confidence spell, but it's also a time spell that will act to help you through the experience and also ensure that it comes along at the right time: when you are ready.

FIRST KISS BLISS SPELL

For girls and boys!
Best day: Friday – ruled by Venus, the planet of love
Best time: Just before dawn (the shift from night to day is good for time magick)
Moon phase: Best during the waxing, but full is good
You will need:
- * 1 large pink candle
- * 1 handful each of lavender and dried rose petals
- * a teaspoon of honey
- * peppermint (if you want to hurry the kiss along)
- * rosemary (if you want to let it take its time)
- * a wind-up clock set to the current time
- * a small bowl of olive oil in which a rose quartz crystal has sat overnight
- * a red ribbon

Assemble everything outside where the sun's first rays can fall on you. If you can't do this, stand near a window where you can see the first light awaken the day.

Cast Circle, preferably with the full ritual, but if you feel sufficiently practised, blast a Circle of Pure Protection.

Place the candle in the centre of Circle and dip your power finger (the index finger of whatever hand you write with) into the oil and with it touch your forehead, lips and heart as you say:

My thoughts are clear, my heart is true, my intent is good and pure.

With your power hand (the one you write with), sprinkle the mixture of lavender and rose petals around the pink candle deosil, i.e. in a sunwise direction (anti-clockwise in the southern hemisphere). The sun should be starting to

lighten the horizon now and, as it does, light the candle
and say:

> *As the sun rises to warm my face,*
> *In perfect time and perfect grace,*
> *So shall my first kiss take its place.*

Repeat this until you feel the warmth of the sun settle
upon you. Now, pick up the clock and if you want your
kiss to happen soon, wind the clock hands forward three
full revolutions as you say:

> *Through time and space speed to me*
> *My perfect kiss easily.*

Now bind the peppermint to the clock with the red
ribbon.

   If you want to take your time, wind the clock hands
backwards three full revolutions as you say:

> *I take my time for peace of mind*
> *When I am ready, the kiss is mine.*

Bind the rosemary to the clock with the red ribbon. Now
place the teaspoon of honey in your mouth. Savour its
sweetness and say:

> *Honey pure, honey sweet,*
> *The perfect kiss is mine to keep.*

The main part of the spell is done but there is a final affirmation – the love spell sealing charm – that requires the most
focus. Stand with your arms outstretched to the sun and
say:

> *I am perfect and whole,*
> *Blessed and essential,*
> *Unlimited is my potential –*
> *My life is unfolding as it must*
> *For the good of all is this magick cast.*

   Then say:

In return for my perfect kiss, I kiss the sun three times twixt.
Spin sunwise three times and blow a kiss to the sun. Snuff
the candle and place it in a box with the clock, the lavender and rose petals. You can cast this spell again to speed
things up or slow things down on the following two
Fridays. By then you will have either done it or the pressure to do it will be off!

I THINK I'M IN LOVE

You are in love with the gorgeous quiet boy or girl at the
back of the classroom, but they don't seem to know you
are alive. You've tried everything, from passing the word
around that you like them, to smiling invitingly at them,
to catching the wrong bus home – the one, coincidentally
enough, they happen to take. But whatever brilliant strat-
egy you come up with, still they will not respond. It's got
to the point now where they are all you think about and
you can't concentrate on your schoolwork. Seeing them
in class is all you look forward to and you are convinced
you're in love with them. But you are a Teen Witch and
have the power, with the right spell, to make them fall in
love with you back – right? WRONG!

Love spells will always backfire or just plain fizzle when
you break the second of the Witches' Laws; 'Do what you
want but don't interfere with another's free will'. As I
explain in the chapter 'Labyrinth of Love' in my first book,
your spell might do an effective job of tying the object of
your affection to you, only for you to find out that the
person's not at all who you thought they were – boring,
selfish or an out-and-out weirdo. But you've woven your
spell so well you can't get rid of them.

Other things can go wrong too. I was watching *Charmed* the other night and one point was actually illustrated quite well. Phoebe and Piper were both lonely and decided they wanted to bring lots of men into their life, so they performed a 'Come to Me' love spell from their Book of Shadows. They went about it in the right way and did not specify a particular person, only asked for certain attributes and qualities that they felt they would like in their partners. They got what they asked for but the spell worked too well. Putting Hollywood special effects and other divorces from reality aside, the show sometimes contains some pretty sound magickal advice such as a point made by Piper in this episode. Phoebe was loving all the attention, (until her boyfriend went obsessively psycho on her), but Piper was not at all happy at how well the spell was working, realising that the conjured-up attention was not real and real human love is far too powerful and profound a force for any spell to capture. After a while all the attention got too much for both our *Charmed* chicks and so they reversed the spell. None of their admirers remembered a thing, proving that it was only the illusion of love.

Before you do any kind of 'come to me' love spell, you should consider doing a self love spell first to make sure that your personal energies are aligned and you are very clear about why you want a partner and what qualities you seek. It's natural for you to experiment in love but you will go through some pretty intense learning curves as far as human interaction goes. All the same, try not to let these changes in your life treat you any harder than they need to. There's so much pressure now on teenagers to grow up quickly, spend your money on looking good (well, magazines' ideas of what looks good) and just about every music video is overloaded with sexy images. This can all be great fun and cool entertainment but the underlying effect can pressure you to keep up and compete with each other, to have the coolest clothes, friends, boyfriends, girlfriends, whatever.

Teen Witches are different from regular teenagers in that they can be aware of all this pressure and decide how much they want to take on and how much they want to stand apart from it. If there's one thing a Witch needs to be able to withstand, it's peer group pressure and the temptation to conform to other people's idea of what our lives should be like. The misinformed sometimes refer to the Craft as a cult, but the reality is that a 'conformist Witch' is an absolute contradiction in terms. Our independence is one of the main sources of our power.

Finding that independence isn't the easiest thing in the world, of course. When I look back at the diaries I kept in my teens, every second paragraph was about some guy and how hard it was to keep him happy first, and keep myself happy second (and every other paragraph was about how fat and ugly I felt). Let me encourage you to enjoy your solo time instead of dedicating your every waking moment to seeking the approval of others. Spend your energies on being the best you can be – perfecting your Witchcraft, doing cool spells and rituals that help and heal the planet, your family, school, your friends and yourself. You will attract people in your life who will teach you the lessons you need to learn.

I have to admit that this is all your classic case of 'do what I say, not as I did'. Unfortunately, absolutely every relationship I had, from my first kiss at fourteen to all the boyfriends I had through my twenties, were pretty much disasters, but this was because I didn't value and respect myself. After a short time of bliss my relationships would descend into destructive, often violent (mentally and emotionally) affairs. A pattern had been set in my early teens: I did not consider myself worthy of love and I attracted people into my life who continued to fit into this vision of life I had for myself. If I had been a Teen Witch then I would have addressed those deep underlying feelings of self-hatred and sadness straight up, and not had to have so many hard lessons to realise I am fine as I am and do deserve love. Now that I've got over those self-destructive thinking patterns, I know I'd rather be single than have a yukky boyfriend. In other words, I've learnt to enjoy and value my own company and that of my friends instead of feeling compelled to sort out someone else's problems, and blaming myself when things go wrong.

The following spell to help you appreciate your own worth is awesome and will leave you feeling amazing if you are feeling uncentred, lonely or just a bit lost in the world. It will reinstate a strong sense of self and what your needs are, and when you are in that 'together' state you can make an enlightened decision as to whether you want to bring a partner into your life or wait for the Universe to get around to it in its own time.

So here's the . . .

AWESOME SELF LOVE SPELL

Do you know the chorus of the song *Scarborough Fair*? ('Are you going to Scarborough Fair? Parsley, sage, rosemary and thyme.') The herbs in the song are for love and healing and this spell uses all four.

Best day: Any (but Friday is good – ruled by Venus, the planet of Love)
Best time: When you need it
Moon phase: Any but preferably waxing or full
You will need:

* a picture of yourself aged between one and five, another aged between five and ten and another aged between ten and now, and a recent picture of yourself.
* a small bunch of parsley
* a small bunch of sage
* a small bunch of rosemary
* a small bunch of thyme
* a lock of your hair
* a silver ribbon if you're a girl, or a gold ribbon if you're a boy
* a silver candle if you're a girl, or a gold candle if you're a boy
* a stick of amber incense
* a sharp knife or pin
* apple cut across to expose the pentacle arrangement of the seeds
* cinnamon
* some beautiful instrumental music

Start the music softly and cast Circle. When you have done this, lay out the four photographs with a different herb lying across each. Carve your full name and your magickal name (if you have one) in your silver or gold candle, lick your thumb and trace it over your name to seal it, then light the wick.

Invoke the Goddess of Love, Aphrodite, and ask for her blessing:

> *Goddess of Love, Aphrodite,*
> *bless me with your glorious presence;*
> *Fuel my self-appreciation,*
> *Fill my soul with sweet elation;*
> *May the waters of your heavenly home*
> *Cleanse my soul and make me whole.*

Sense Aphrodite manifesting in your Circle as a swirling pink sea of light – in your mind's eye you may see her float in on her shell. Know that she is here to magnify your finest qualities and bring out the very best in you.

Now pick up the apple (which is sacred to Aphrodite) and sprinkle some cinnamon on it (for purification and strength). Now slowly eat the apple and be aware that you are taking in Aphrodite's power. When you are finished, save five seeds and put them aside.

Now pick up the bunches of herbs and, placing the lock of your hair in the centre, wind the ribbon around the stem five times and tie a big bow as you say:

> *I weave the strands of my life together,*
> *With these sacred herbs I bless my endeavours.*
> *I am good, I am whole,*
> *I am proud to be me,*
> *I share this love with the world.*

Inhale deeply the pungent scent of your herb charm as you look at the photos of your progression in life as a growing, evolving human being. Feel a deep, unconditional sense of appreciation for yourself and where you've come from and where you're going. If you feel your mind wandering and settling on unpleasant memories, focus on Aphrodite's perfect pink presence inside you and around you in your Circle, breathing in her pink light, feeling it enter your lungs, warm and loving.

Now say the Love spell sealing charm:
I am perfect and whole,
Blessed and essential,
Unlimited is my potential.
My life is unfolding as it must,
For the good of all is this magick cast.

When you are ready, thank the Goddess Aphrodite for her assistance and close Circle. Take the five apple seeds outside and plant them as an offering to the eternally renewing forces of life and hang your bunch of herbs in your window or somewhere they can dry and be kept for as long as you like, or until you do the spell again.

OK, you've done the Awesome Self Love Spell and you still want that guy or girl. There's no way around it, so here's . . .

THE 'I HAVE TO HAVE YOU' SPELL

As I mentioned above, it's not a good idea to try to attract a particular individual in case your judgement of them isn't all that accurate. After all, you're obviously not that close to them or you wouldn't be needing this spell. Instead what you need to do is look at what attracts you to them and define all those scrumptious qualities that you perceive them to have (be aware you're often looking at them through rose coloured glasses).

As a Teen I used to get crushes on famous people – and funnily enough, because of my work, I've met quite a few of them and they've turned out to be a long way from the perfect creatures I thought they were. In fact, a couple of them have been horrible! It's disappointing when you find out that the person who wrote and performed your ultra-favourite song is a loser – but that's life sometimes in the world of music! Having said that, some I've met are nicer than I ever imagined them to be. People are people with good and bad points, no matter whether they're a Number One pop artist or the gardener.

Anyway, this spell works to draw to you your perfect partner.

Best day: Again Friday (ruled by Venus, the planet of Love)

Best time: The early evening

Moon phase: It would be perfect when the new crescent moon makes her first appearance of the month in the sky, but anytime during the crescent and before full is good.

You will need:

* a strawberry herbal tea bag
* a pink candle
* pink, rose or mixed flower scented bath salts, or maybe a bath bomb (Lush make an excellent one for this spell in the shape of a heart with nine rose buds embedded in it.)
* rose potpourri
* a pink cord, 33 cm long (you could buy silky,

present-wrapping cord from the newsagency)
* ¼ cup olive oil that a rose has floated in overnight
* a piece of paper and a pink texta
* a white cup filled with nearly boiled water

As a part of the ritual, before casting Circle light the pink
candle and take a bath using the bath salts as you drink the
cup of strawberry tea from the white cup. As you soak,
meditate on the qualities of your ideal partner. If a particular person enters your mind, think about what you like
about them, then let their image float away. When you feel
focused and ready, get out of the bath and carry your candle
to where you're doing your ritual (try not to let the flame
blow out if it's lit). Then, cast Circle and invoke Aphrodite:

Aphrodite, bring me perfect love
For the good of all, with harm to none.

On your piece of paper write down all the things you want
in your dream partner – not just personality qualities, you
can even specify hair colour or eye colour (just don't think
of a specific person!). When you are ready, put the paper
down and sprinkle a little of the potpourri on it as you say:

Flower of love,
Bless my request,
Manifest the person
That will suit me best.

Do this two more times so you have recited the charm
three times in total. Now, fold the paper around the potpourri to contain it inside.

Next, pick up the cord and tie five knots, spacing them
evenly. As you tie them you must focus clearly on your
desired person coming to you.

Tie the first knot at the right end of the cord and say:
By one, this spell's begun.
Trace a pentagram with a little of the rose-infused olive oil on the knot. Then tie the next:
By two, it shall come true.
Trace another pentagram on this knot; then tie the next:
By three, So Mote it be.
Trace another pentagram and tie another knot:
By four, for the good of all.
Trace another pentagram, and tie another knot:
By five, love comes alive.
And trace a pentagram on the final knot.

You now have created a magickal cord which is charged with your spell.

Thank the Goddess Aphrodite and close the Circle. Take the cord and put it somewhere safe with your folded piece of paper (maybe you could place both in a clean, white, cotton pillowcase and put them away in a drawer). When your new love arrives on the scene, you need to release the magick of the cord and burn it. Place the cord on the ground and trace a pentagram in the air over each knot (without touching it) as you say each time, 'This magick is released, the spell has done its work.' When you've done all five, burn the cord. You can burn the paper charm with the cord.

I think it's important to release the magick of this spell once it has worked because you want to allow the other person's input and energy to take your relationship further, and in new directions that perhaps you hadn't thought of. If you have really fixed ideas about how you think a relationship should be, you won't grow as a person. As much as I've had some hard, sad times I have benefited from my different relationships. As the negative patterns of the past gradually shifted, and whatever their good and bad points might have been, all my partners showed me things about myself that ultimately led me to becoming a better and happier person.

Just a note, you can adapt the above spell to bring a best friend, or just more friends, into your life. As you do the spell think about what you would like in a friend, what things you would like to do together, and fun times you would like to share. When you invoke the Goddess Aphrodite ask her to 'bring me perfect friendship'.

ROSE POTPOURRI – MAKE YOUR OWN!

Pluck the petals from about five lovely big scented red roses and spread them over waxed paper in a dry, warm place. When they are completely dry, sprinkle them with two tablespoons of orris root and with your hands mix it all up together in a glass bowl. As you do this, visualise pink light streaming from your hands into the bowl as you say over and over, 'Love, love, love'. Finally, a few drops of rose oil mixed in will enhance the scent and seal in strong love-attracting power.

UNCONDITIONAL LOVE SPELL

This is a spell to do for anyone just because you love them. They could be your best friend, your sister or brother, your teacher, or your girlfriend or boyfriend. This spell works to send them lots of positive energy and it also lets the Universe know how special this person is and so attracts good fortune to them.

Best time: anytime!
You will need:
 * a light blue candle
 * lavender oil
 * a sugar cube
 * a really beautiful flower in a vase
 * a pin

Cast Circle and trace the name of your loved one into the candle, lick your thumb and trace over the name. Light the candle and place just one drop of oil on the sugar cube as you say:

> *For love and friendship, pure and sweet.*

Now pop it in the vase with the flower. Hold the vase and gaze at the flower as you say:

> *Universe, I ask (their name) be blessed.*
> *She/He fills my life with happiness;*
> *Return to them three times three*
> *The pleasure they have given me.*

Now close Circle and give the flower to your special person. If it's impossible to give it to them, keep it in the vase yourself and think of them every time you look at it.

SIMPLE SPELL TO ENJOY SINGLE LIFE

Sometimes you can feel really left out when all your friends have boyfriends or girlfriends and you don't. In addition to the Awesome Self Love Spell, here's an easy one to help you feel happy and empowered.

Best time: whenever you need it.

You will need:
* a feather
* a clear quartz crystal
* a white velvet or other cloth drawstring pouch
* a white candle
* a glass of spring water
* a piece of white paper
* a silver pen

For this spell you're going to make an amulet. This can be done in a fully-cast Circle or if you prefer, snap up a Pure Power Shield. Either way, make sure you empower your objects (see 'Hot Spell Tips' in this book).

Light the candle, and hold the crystal, and say:

My mind is clear for my intent.

Drop the crystal in the water, take a sip and say:

My life is mine, my goals are met.

Now, on the paper draw a pentagram with a circle around it touching the five points and around that write your full name. Take the white feather and trace over the pentagram three times with it as you say:

Feather of air and star of earth,
Empower me as fire burns;
I am free, my will flows deep;
No need to be in another's keep.

Snuff the candle, put the feather in the bag with the paper (you can fold it up), pour the water onto a plant and pop the crystal in the bag too. Snap off the Power Shield.

Keep your amulet with you so that you can hold it and repeat the charm whenever you're feeling lonely or left out.

Let's Talk About Teen Sex

Writing about Teen sexuality is always one of those risky things. If you put one foot wrong, you get jumped up and down on as a corrupter of youth – and if you happen to be a Witch, you're doubly vulnerable since a lot of people are hostile to that as well. So before continuing, here's the score: I haven't written this chapter to tell you how to run your sexual lives, when to begin them or what other choices you ought to be making on the subject. What I'd like you to think about is the fact that your body and your sexuality are your own and it's not up to anybody – your friends, family and definitely not an author you've probably never met – to tell you what you should be doing with them.

That doesn't mean you should disregard all advice automatically, a practice as robotic and self-negating as doing everything you're told without question. If you're still pretty young, it's a safe bet that your parents will have some pretty heavy duty opinions on your sexual behaviour. Because a lot of parents are uncomfortable discussing the topic with their kids, they often express these opinions as a stack of completely black and white, thou-shalts and thou-shalt-nots which tend to disregard your own feelings. The challenge for you in that situation is to keep in mind that, however their opinions might be expressed, you can be pretty sure that they're motivated by concerns for your health, safety and happiness. Perhaps they're trying to protect you from making some of the bad choices they made at your age. A lot of teens end up making precisely those same mistakes (or much worse ones) by automatically rebelling against ultimatums from their parents. So, before you make any decision on your own sexual life, be very clear that you're not falling into that trap.

The same thing applies when your friends try to make your choices for you by telling you you're being a wimp or a spoilsport or a loser for behaving in a certain way around sexual issues. Every time you make a decision on this subject, be one hundred percent clear who's making that decision: Is it you? Or someone you're giving your power of choice away to?

Having said that, I do have a few strong recommendations about your sexual life. The main one is simply to educate yourself on the subject as much as you possibly can. It's not the place of this book to be a sex education manual but there's a stack of really helpful information out there so make it your business to soak it up (for somewhere to start, I've included some contact details for associations you may like to contact at the end of this chapter). For Witches, sexuality is always held to be a powerful and sacred thing but just because you might be a Teen Witch doesn't mean you're safe from the dangers out there in the sexual world.

Find out all you can about safe sex, contraception and, just as importantly, how to treat your future (or maybe even present) lovers with respect, kindness and understanding and how to ensure you're treated the same way. I suppose the first thing to realise is that it's illegal to have sex until you are sixteen years old, so you should bear this in mind whenever you are making decisions about your sexuality.

All of the above applies to all teens, of course, but here are a few tips for those who also have the advantages of being able to whip up a little magick! The following are some spells to deal with some of the really big events that will confront you as you awaken sexually.

BODY AWARENESS

I spent so much time torturing myself about my appearance when I was a teen. I had no bosoms and my lips were too big (my nickname at school was 'Fish Lips'). When I left school and started work as a model/receptionist for a clothing company, all of a sudden I was too fat. And when I started having sex, I was even more hyper-critical of myself. I used to turn around and look at my bum in the mirror and *hate* it. There is so much pressure on young girls, and increasing pressure on young boys, to conform to particular body types – the kinds of bodies that only a tiny fraction of the human race have naturally, and only a slightly larger fraction of the human race can achieve with masses of ridiculously hard work. At a time of supposed enlightenment and liberation in the scheme of human evolution, never has there been so much insidious mind programming in the world of advertising and so many disempowering messages in the shows we watch on television about what our bodies should be like.

Teen Witches need to have a good hard think about how much they want to absorb from the world around them about how they should look. For a start, the three girls from *Charmed* are portrayed as powerful Witches but they are all skinny as rakes (Prue especially) with big bosoms, dressed in designer clothing and looking as fresh as daisies whether they're waking up, going to a nightclub or zapping a demon. Buffy and Willow barely ooze a drop of sweat when vanquishing vampires; Sandra Bullock and Nicole Kidman didn't have an ounce of excess fat between them in *Practical Magic* and even older Witches in movies like *The Witches of Eastwick* tend to get portrayed by the likes of Susan Sarandon, Michelle Pfeiffer and Cher – all very beautiful, and very thin!

As a Witch, you need to be able to value your physical self whatever shape, age or state of health it might be in. While not every Witch needs to work skyclad (naked) in shared Circles if she or he chooses not to, every Witch should be able to stand skyclad in front of a full length mirror and respect and love what's reflected back. If that reflection causes embarrassment, anger or even disgust, your magick will always be diminished. All spells and rituals require the Witch to say, either actually or metaphorically, at some point: 'As I will so mote it be.' If there's some part of that 'I', that sense of yourself, that you can't respect, there's no way your powers can be firing on all cylinders. Besides which, if you allow the media's idea of the right shape or features for a human being to poison your respect for your own body, you're falling for one of the oldest con tricks on the planet: if you give in to feeling like an under-achiever, you'll keep spending money to try either to catch up or to compensate (and this is exactly what the media, or advertisers, want!). Once again, it's your choice whether you want to believe this or not.

As a performer myself, I guess I could be accused of being part of the same conspiracy, but let me assure you that just about every photo you've seen of me has been airbrushed to the max (it's all makeup and lighting, darling!) Seriously, you might look at my photo on the cover of this book and think that I scrub up pretty well. I know I am attractive but what I hope I'm projecting is a sense of confidence and comfort in my body. Sometimes if I'm around other people when I'm feeling down, no-one gives me a second look (except maybe to think, 'Why is Fiona sitting there with such a grumpy look on her face?'). At other times I will be feeling confident and happy and I can't get the boys off me!

To some extent I do have to present myself in a certain way to be able to do my job but the last thing I'd want is to give the impression that I believe we should all try to look a certain way either as Witches or simply as people. The most lasting and extraordinary beauty in these artificial, commercial times is that which comes from within – that inner light and sense of pride an individual has within themselves. Our bodies are the lampshade, our spirit is the light that shines. Are you a 20 watt bulb or a 100 watt bulb?

THE 100 WATT LIGHT BULB SPELL

Best time: a waxing to full moon
Best day: Thursday, ruled by Jupiter and good for confidence

You will need:
* ✳ a cup of Bright Water (see page 164)
* ✳ a full length mirror
* ✳ a torch
* ✳ four white candles
* ✳ to be skyclad for this spell!

Cast Circle and then set up the four white candles to form a circle in front of your mirror. Turn the lights off and light the candles. Sprinkle the Bright Water around you deosil (sunwise, or anticlockwise in the southern hemisphere). Dip your power finger (or your athame) in the Bright Water and trace a pentagram on your third eye, over your heart, and over your solar plexus (between your belly button and bottom of your ribcage).

Shine the torch on your third eye as you look at your-self in the mirror and say:

> *(Your name), you are bright to see;*
> *In your light no shadows be;*
> *The fire of the sun,*
> *The glow of the moon,*
> *The sparkle of stars,*
> *All flow from you.*

Now shine the torch over your heart (not the reflection) and repeat the incantation, then over your solar plexus, and repeat the incantation.

When you have done this, look in the mirror and use the torch to trace a large pentagram of light in front of you (fast so that the light of the torch blurs and seems to draw solid lines). Raise power in whatever way you like (a good method is to hold your hands over your heart and chant your own name over and over, and feel your body heat light up as all the inner beauty you have gets revved up

and charges to the surface). When you feel the power
peaking, throw your hands into the air and say:

I am divine, shining light;
I am Goddess, (or God depending on whether you're
a girl or a boy)
Pure and bright,
From stop to go,
I switch on my beauty glow (or 'hot glow', 'spunk glow',
'inner glow' – whatever term does it for you!)

Stand with your arms in the air, exulting in your glowing
self. When you are ready, close Circle. Every morning, after
washing, dip your finger in the Bright Water and trace a
pentagram over your heart to help your inner beauty glow
all day.

BRIGHT WATER

You will need:
* a cup of orange blossom flowers (if you can't get these,
  peel the skin of two oranges and cut into small pieces)
* one cup spring water
* three drops of frankincense oil (this is expensive so if you
  can't afford it buy pure frankincense incense sticks and
  stir the mixture with three of these)
* three pinches of dragon's blood powder (you can buy this
  cheaply at the suppliers suggested in the back of this
  book, but if you can't get it, in your mortar and pestle
  crush five crystals of rock salt together with a pinch of
  cinnamon and a pinch of nutmeg
* one clear quartz crystal
* orange food dye

Soak the flowers or peel in the spring water overnight in a
glass. Strain the liquid in the morning and add the oil (or stir

for five minutes with the incense sticks), then sprinkle in the dragon's blood powder (or your alternative). Drop the crystal in and add three drops of the dye. Hold the glass in both hands and say:

Crystal of light,
Charge this water
With moonlight and wisdom,
Sunshine and laughter.

BODY SACRED SPELL

I mentioned the disaster of my first kiss in 'Teen Witch in Love'. Well, things didn't get dramatically better after that complete dud of a first experience. I was petrified the first time I had sex and for at least the next year after. I used to lie there in the 'starfish' position with my older boyfriend on top of me saying, 'Can't you move, can't you do something?' I would reply, 'What am I supposed to do?' I don't recall him ever offering any particularly helpful advice at that point. Apart from not knowing some of the elementary physical tips for young lovers, my real problem was that I had no concept of my self-worth and the sacredness of my body. I was just trying to fit in and do what I thought a 'girlfriend' was supposed to do.

The whole thing was like the First Kiss Fiasco Part Two! I felt a lot of pressure to have sex, at a time when I honestly didn't feel ready to. Everyone else was telling me they were doing it and I thought I had to, as well. I was dating this guy at the time. He was twenty-two and I was fifteen and absolutely smitten with him. I was quite innocent, getting swept up in the churning sea of hormones inside me, but not really thinking of the ramifications of flirting with an adult.

My moment of reckoning came in the back seat of his Torana in a national park in Sydney. For that added touch of romance and intimacy, we had tea towels hung in the windows. All of a sudden our kisses turned into a massive grope session (him groping me, and me sort of putting up with it) and then before I knew it my pants were off and he was doing IT. Well, at least, he was trying to and not actually succeeding. I was a virgin and had never even used a tampon, and it wasn't going to be that easy. Thankfully he stopped and didn't force me any more than he had already.

I'm only telling you all that so, if it's not too late, you might be able to make some much better choices than I did on that huge step in my life.

I had been brought up to fear and suppress the natural urges inside me, so they exploded at all the wrong moments. If I had been a Teen Witch I would have thought long and hard about my first sexual experience. I would have been in touch with the sacredness of my body and approached the whole experience completely differently. For a start I would never have done it with that loser! But I was just trying to fit in and be cool – all my girlfriends thought it was great that I was dating an older guy. If any of them are reading this now, at last they'll know just how 'great' it actually was.

Here is the Body Sacred Spell, which you can do to strengthen your sense of self, so that you will make the right choice for your first time. It can also help you if you've already had a disappointing first experience and want to make sure the next time is way, way better.

Best day: Friday (Venus again!)

Best time: evening before bed

You will need:
* ✳ sacred self bath salts (see page 168)
* ✳ purple candle
* ✳ purple paper
* ✳ gold pen
* ✳ sharp pin

Run a bath and cast Circle in the bathroom. Trace a pentagram, your sun sign symbol (in other words, your 'star sign') and your name and age on the candle with the pin. Lick your thumb and seal the carving with your spit, then dip your finger in a little rose geranium oil and trace over the pentagram with it.

Pour the sacred self bath salts in the water and stir deosil (anticlockwise in the southern hemisphere) in a big circle seven times with your power hand as you say:

> *Mystic be the number seven*
> *I call upon the powers of heaven*
> *To bless and manifest my goal:*
> *Perfect harmony body and soul;*
> *As is my will so it will be,*
> *For the good of all but most for me.*

Get in the bath and soak – feel the water caress every pore of your body and know that you are utterly unique and deserve only the very best in what you choose to experience. Meditate on this, and when you are ready, get out of the bath, write on the purple paper your name and underneath it the pentagram, and then the following:

> *I, (name), declare*
> *That I am a child of the Goddess and God*
> *I am special and proud, holy and good;*
> *My first time (or next time if you've already done it and you*
> *want to improve on the next experience), will be a rite, one of*

> *truth and bliss,*
> *An expression of love that is*
> *Mine to enjoy and mine to give.*

Close Circle, and for the next six nights before going to sleep, burn the candle and read your declaration. Keep both the candle and paper wrapped in cloth (maybe a nice big white linen hanky) when you're not working the spell. This spell can be redone regularly, but it is good to perform it when you think you've met someone you really like and you might be considering taking the plunge.

SACRED SELF BATH SALTS

You will need:

* ¾ cups of semi-ground rock salt
* ¼ cup Epsom salts (from the chemist)
* purple food dye (from the supermarket)
* essential oil of rose geranium (it's about $10 a bottle – but it's worth investing in because it smells divine and can be burnt in an oil burner to help continue the spell working)
* verbena (also called vervain – a herb you can buy at the health food store)
* chamomile (also at your health food store)

Grind the two herbs in your mortar and pestle until they are mostly powdery. As you grind say this chant:

> *Herbs of power, herbs of worth,*
> *Assist me in my magick work.*

Mix the rock and Epsom salts together and drop in a few drops of the food dye. Give it a good shake as the salt absorbs the colour. Mix through the herbs, and drop in five drops of the oil and mix it through. (A good trick is to put it all in a waxed paper bag and shake it around.)

OOPS . . . I DID IT AGAIN!

Recently a young male friend of mine asked if he could discuss with me a 'problem' he was having with me. He was seventeen and dating a sixteen-year-old girl that he really liked but he was having so much trouble with sex. He could not do it for more than a few seconds before he came and got really embarrassed. She would feel disappointed and embarrassed too. They would try – but the same thing would happen again.

I told him his 'problem' of premature ejaculation was totally natural and most teenage guys experience it. It has to do with nerves and the pressure to perform. Girls, of course, suffer from the same pressures but for them the reaction is the reverse and they often don't reach orgasm at all. I didn't orgasm with a partner until I was nineteen.

I encouraged him to stop having sex with her for a while and to focus on building up other areas of their relationship – like doing fun things together, having lots of yummy cuddles and kisses, and talking about their hopes and dreams. I also suggested the next spell for him to try. A few weeks later he called me and said the problem was solved! When the pressure to perform was off and he could relax, he felt more comfortable and the spell worked to align the energies of his head and heart so that he could feel integrated and in touch with his body.

THE IT'S ALL GOOD SPELL

Day: Sunday
Time: Sunrise
You will need:
* a gold candle

* frankincense resin (available from the occult supply stores listed at the back – the resin is not that expensive, about $8 for a small bag)
* charcoal disc (most health food stores sell them, as well as occult supply and New Age stores. See the Tips section for how to light them.)
* a plate filled with sand (you need roughly a 20 cm circle of sand, a couple of centimetres thick)

As the sun rises, cast Circle and light the gold candle. Light the charcoal disc and drop a pinch of frankincense on it. With your athame or power finger, trace your name in the sand and then a circle three times in a deosil/sunwise direction around it. As you do this chant:

> *In light of the mighty sun,*
> *I align myself to the powers above;*
> *I am great, I am good;*
> *All exists as it should.*

Sprinkle a few more grains of frankincense on the disc and say:

As is my will, So Mote It Be,
The spell is cast – one, two, three.

Clap your hands or strike your bell or gong as you count 'one, two, three'.

Sit for a while, enjoying the sunrise and sprinkling grains of frankincense on the disc as an offering to the Sun. When you are ready close Circle and don't worry – it's all good!

ORGASMS

I got into heaps of trouble when I was busted masturbating in my bedroom when I was nine. It was fire cracker night (when they were still legal in NSW) and I was bored waiting for my family to leave to attend a big bonfire and party that was going on in my suburb. I had been masturbating for a while by that time in my life and I always was very careful to be extremely discreet, because I was told that 'playing with yourself' was really bad. However, on this night Mum walked in on me and, after looking at me in horror, sent Dad in to tell me off. He very helpfully told me that it was a sin and dirty and said, 'It's bad to do it.' I remember saying, 'But it feels so nice', which in retrospect probably wasn't very tactful in the circumstances – but I was genuinely confused. All I knew was that I had discovered a wonderful thing which I could do all by myself, and which made me feel like I had magick inside me. Which is precisely what it was.

Sex and sexuality are the most natural things for humans and absolutely essential parts of our lives – in fact, it is the only reason we are alive. If sexual pleasure wasn't so blissful the human race would have died out before we were out of the trees! In other words we humans have a wonderful ability to feel intense physical joy and for many people orgasm is about as close to spiritual ecstasy as they'll reach in their lives. It isn't just a pleasure like eating when you're hungry, or resting when you're tired. It's a fire that makes you feel at one with the forces of all life and creativity. When I orgasm, as a Witch I feel all the joy that churns at the very centre of the Universe. I feel utterly divine and blessed and transcendent (which is why I sometimes use orgasm as a solo power-raising method in ritual). This couldn't be further from what I was taught as a young Catholic, that sex and orgasm should be suppressed and considered 'dirty', and shrouded in fear.

All acts of love and pleasure are sacred to the Goddess. A Teen Witch understands this, and the deeply sacred and divine nature of their bodies, and knows they have nothing to feel ashamed or even confused about. They are beautiful, perfect and loved by the Goddess and God as an expression of the brilliant and powerful force of life. Orgasm is a sacred gift, as well as being one of the coolest and most fun things to do – it's free and easily available! (Having said that, if you have trouble orgasming, then don't stress, take your time, keep practising and it will work itself out.)

The only other thing I'd like to add on the subject of masturbation is that every time you do it you're tapping into a great source of magickal energy which you might as well use some of the time, instead of just frittering it away, however pleasantly. A sacred orgasm ritual is very simple. Just do it! Don't be in too much of a rush (that sets a bad precedent for later life, especially for guys!). Don't let anyone make you feel guilty or worried about doing it. And dedicate each beautiful feeling you have to someone or something special in the Universe.

Oh, and a final tip, do a Private Space spell so you don't get interrupted by people barging into your room without knocking!

THE PINK WITCH

At its core, Witchcraft embraces the magnificent diversity of humanity in all its colours, shapes, sizes and preferences. We encourage evolution and change and one of the most dynamic modern aspects of the Craft is its challenging of patriarchal gender roles.

Witchcraft is a religion which honours the Life Force as sacred and is primarily matriarchal, though many Wiccans are tending more and more to a Taoist-like balance of female and male energy. The Goddess is still often given extra emphasis but that's largely to help correct the imbalance of the masculine over the feminine, which many of our cultures have. However, as the gap between men and women's power in society becomes narrower, the need to exult the Goddess above the God becomes less necessary. Witches also do not see the emotional and physical union of heterosexual couples as superior to that of lesbian and gay couples. Love and pleasure are sacred to Witches and all Witches are free to explore these in whatever way they choose. Reproduction of the species is not the only expression of love or pleasure, nor the only form of fertility. We acknowledge that absolute masculinity and femininity exist only in the abstract. In practice, each of us has male and female elements to our personality and energy. Not surprisingly, gay and bisexual culture took the rainbow as the symbol of the richness of variety in our species.

The polarities of male and female qualities exist in both sexes—the human being is a complex animal! Ancient Eastern religion comments on this: in Taoism there is a concept expressed as the 'Ten Thousand Things', in which nothing is purely Yin or purely Yang, but rather a complex blend of the two: not black, not white, but grey. Also, consider the actual Taoist symbols of Yin and Yang—each contains the essence of its opposite.

In many ways, especially in the past, Witches and homosexuals have a lot in common. Throughout history, both groups have often been treated as outcasts and minorities to be hunted down and persecuted. In these modern times, Witches and homosexuals have been increasingly encouraged to come out of our individual 'closets' (for a Witch, the broom closet, of course!), and though there is still prejudice directed at us, there is considerably more freedom for us to express ourselves.

In fact, prior to the dominance of the Western patriarchal religious mindset, there is a rich history of the profound role the homosexual has played in the spiritual evolution of humanity. It is only since the Christian era that the idea of a woman or effeminate man as a spiritual leader has been denigrated (funny, though, isn't it, that priests seem to still have a fondness for long flowing skirts?!).

In ancient temples and primitive cultures the homosexual, effeminate man and virgin Priestess (virgin meaning complete unto herself) were all seen to have great psychic and magickal abilities. Also, if you do a bit of research you'll find many of the Goddesses and Gods of old had lesbian and gay encounters. Hermes, the Greek God of magick, medicine, intelligence and communication was portrayed as androgynous and bisexual. And going further back in time to one of the greatest ancient Syrian Gods, Baal was often portrayed as being one with his female counterpart, Astarte, and invoked as 'Baal—whether God or Goddess'.

The infamous isle of Lesbos was colonised by Amazons in the 6th century BCE. The women of this island were revered as poets, musicians, artists, lovers and Priestesses in service of the great Greek Goddesses, Artemis and Aphrodite. Even though during the early Christian era most traces of this colony were destroyed, today some Wiccan covens exist as female-only—the roles within the coven being based on the perceived structure and function of these ancient temples.

Some traditions in the Craft teach that energy polarity is like a battery and to raise power during magickal ritual it is essential to have the 'opposites' of male and female acting together. But these energies are given gender-specific definitions based on archetypal behaviour and roles of women and men in our society, not on some profound universal truth of what it is to be male and female. We all have the Goddess and God within us. A perfect example of this is raising power as a solitary Witch—when firing up alone, you are expounding on the totality of your personal being, celebrating the fact that all things exist within as well as without.

In Witchcraft, gay, lesbian, bisexual and transgendered humans can find a sense of spiritual peace and integration. There are inspiring role models, Gods and Goddesses to relate to, and a tolerant and compassionate magickal community to be a part of. Everyone can turn the Wheel of the Year, dance the spiral dance of the Cosmos and take their rightful place as divine children of the Universe.

Contact Phone Numbers

Here are some contact details for any queries or questions you have about sex, and your sexuality:

ACT
Family Planning Association (02) 6247 3077.
Gay Information and Counselling (02) 6247 2726.
NSW
Family Planning Association (02) 9716 6099.
Gay and Lesbian Counselling (02) 9207 2800.
NORTHERN TERRITORY
Family Planning Association (08) 8948 0144.
Crisis Line (08) 8922 7156.
QUEENSLAND
Family Planning Association (07) 3252 5151.
Lesbian Line (07) 3839 3277; Gayline (07) 3839 3277.
SOUTH AUSTRALIA
Family Planning Association (08) 8431 5177.
Gay and Lesbian Counselling (08) 8362 3223.
TASMANIA
Family Planning Association (03) 6228 5244.
Gay Information Service (03) 6234 8179.
VICTORIA
Family Planning Association (03) 9257 0100.
Gay and Lesbian Switchboard (03) 9510 5488.
WESTERN AUSTRALIA
Family Planning Association (08) 9227 6177.
Gay and Lesbian Counselling (08) 9328 9044.
NEW ZEALAND
Youthline National Freephone 0800 376 633.

Out Of It

Drugs – well, what can I say besides the obvious: 'Don't do it'? In *Witch – A Personal Journey*, the chapter 'Flying High' talks about why drugs and magick don't mix for older Witches and that goes triple for Teen Witches. I'm not saying this to be straight or to sound like a mum or dad. I'm saying this because I know – I've been there and done it . . . and it didn't help my Witchcraft one little bit.

Witchcraft is demanding and challenging and often when you get it happening in a big way the rush is better than any artificial high you could experience on drugs. With Witchcraft there's no come down, no health problems and it's relatively free. It won't make you do things you regret either.

Alcohol is something most Teens at one time or another will experiment with, and even abuse. Alcohol and cigarettes cause more grief, illness and death than just about anything else and yet are legal and promoted to the max!

But Teen Witches with even half a brain don't drink anything alcoholic, and don't breath in anything but incense. For cigarettes, the first, most obvious reason is that they pollute the environment; the second is that they kill you and the people around you; and the third is that if you buy them, you are supporting huge multinational corporations who are responsible for massive amounts of ecological damage. Plus smoking is disgusting and looks stupid (in my opinion). And most importantly, it makes you completely unkissable!

And alcohol . . . well, I remember the first time I got drunk. I was fourteen and there was a school dance, and surprise, surprise – I was actually allowed to go! My group of friends decided to meet at the basketball court first to get smashed before we went in. I sculled half a 'goonie bag' (the silver foil bag inside a wine cask) of very cheap moselle. I didn't really want to do it but everyone else was having some and I always overdid things in an attempt to impress people so that hopefully they'd like me.

We started walking down to the school hall and all of a sudden I felt like I was floating, and started giggling uncontrollably. Now you may be thinking, 'cool, that sounds like fun' – but half an hour later the scene was anything but. I ended up in the lap of an older boy pashing him in front of everyone, then I got busted by the headmistress, Sister Cecelia, and she called my parents. I had to sit outside to wait for them to pick me up early, and when they arrived I threw up in the gutter. It was not cool – not only was I grounded for months, I was branded a slut at school.

As I explain in 'Teen Witch in Love', I was actually quite shy, especially when it came to this kind of stuff – so I was devastated. I couldn't believe I'd done something so stupid. In fact, I barely remembered doing it at all.

If I had been a Teen Witch at that age I would have had a lot more respect for myself and my body. I wouldn't have felt the need to show off and try to impress my friends, and what's more, I would have had a great night. (My friends who stayed on said the night was unreal.)

But unfortunately my stupidity didn't end there. Six months later it was suggested it would be best for me to leave my school because I got caught taking pills. One of my friends' dad was a musician who toured on the road a lot and had pills called Avils for car sickness. I took a handful of them and was found wandering around the schoolyard in a daze when I was supposed to be in my science class. Again, I did it to impress a tough gang of girls who I hoped would stop picking on me. But, no, they just thought I was an idiot and I got expelled.

This totally sucked – my already precarious relationship with my parents was trashed and they were utterly heart-broken. My sister and brother were really embarrassed to be related to me and my teen hell just descended into even deeper depths of despair.

So many of the dumb things I did were because of peer pressure and just me needing to feel like I was someone special and belonged somewhere. If I'd been practising the Craft back then, I would have known I was both these things already and would never have made my life so difficult for myself.

There is an enormous amount of pressure on teens to be cool and fit in and sometimes it might feel easier to just say, 'OK, I will'. But you will most likely be fitting into a scene that's not going to do you any favours and certainly not give you a leg-up into being a awesome person – it will just be wasting your time when you could be doing something ultimately far more rewarding. Basically if you think that cigarettes make you cooler, visit a lung cancer ward. If you feel drinking alcohol will improve your life, ask a family who've lost a loved one in a drink-driving accident. If you believe illegal drugs will make you happier, talk to someone who's wasted years of their life trying to get straight again, or anyone who's done time in a prison on a drugs charge. Well, call me prejudiced again but I've got a theory that teenagers who are drawn to the Craft are probably more together than most and don't need to do any of those things. It's enough to imagine the number of people out there who'd give anything to change places with a healthy young person who hasn't destroyed their fitness, their happiness and their freedom through addictions they could so easily have avoided.

But just in case, here's a couple of spells to help you focus and avoid situations that you'd rather not be in.

JUST SAY NUP SPELL

Best time: either a Saturday during the waning moon
(or when you need it)

You will need:

* ✳ one black candle
* ✳ one lemon
* ✳ one knife
* ✳ hot black tea
* ✳ one ice cube
* ✳ black cloth

Cast Circle either with the full ritual or an Instant Circle
of Pure Protection. Light the black candle and carve the
name of the problem (e.g., drugs, or a particular person
who is trying to make you take drugs, etc.) into the side
of the lemon with the knife. Then, using all your powers
of visualisation, imagine the problem, and when you have
a clear image in your mind take a sip of the tea and blow
five hot breaths over the lemon as you say forcefully:

(problem) I sour your power over me,
You now have no hold on me;
I am free, my resolve is great,
I have the power to decide my fate.

Now snuff the candle. Open the Circle and take the candle,
lemon (wrapped in black cloth as you transport it) and the
ice (you could use a thermos to keep it frozen if you have
to travel a way). Go to where the problem occurs – at your
school, at the bus stop, in the person's street. Unwrap the
lemon and bury it as close as you can to the problem place.
Stand the black candle on the earth and light it, saying the
incantation again. When you have done this, put the ice in
your mouth and then blow five cold breaths on the earth

under which the lemon lies, with the final breath blowing
out the candle. As the lemon rots, so will your problem
recede.

NATURALLY HIGH SPELL

This is a spell you can do before you go out so that you
are feeling naturally buzzed!

You will need:
  * ylang ylang essential oil (a bottle is about $18
    but well worth the investment)
  * one orange candle
  * one yellow candle
  * one feather
  * one chalice (beautiful glass or goblet)
  * berry juice (either strawberry, blackberry,
    cranberry etc., or a mixture)
  * honey
  * a silver spoon

Cast Circle, either with the full or instant ritual.

Light the candles and take a few deep breaths as you
gaze at the flames to calm and centre yourself. Now stir
half a teaspoon of honey in the berry juice deosil (sunwise,
or anti-clockwise in the southern hemisphere) and, as you
do, repeat faster and faster the following incantation as you
stir until you feel the powers in the cup peaking:

Love, joy, power grows,
This magick brew does bestow.

(Watch out – it's a bit of a tongue twister!)

Now drink the juice until it is finished, feeling its magickal charge send a buzz through your body. Next, place
three drops of ylang ylang on the feather and, fanning it
in front of your face, deeply inhale its divine scent.

Then, holding the feather out in front of you, trace a large Witches' pentagram in the air and step through it; then turn around, trace another and step through it; and then once again, turn around and do the same.

Holding the feather above your head, say:

> *Three times blessed am I,*
> *Powerful and naturally high.*
> *(You can say 'super-naturally high' if you like!)*
> *My charm is great,*
> *My intent is good,*
> *This time is mine, be as it should.*

Touch the feather to your third eye (between the eyebrows), throat and heart. Close Circle and if you like, wear some of the ylang ylang oil as perfume – it's great for girls and guys. Be careful, however, if you have sensitive skin: mix a few drops in a teaspoon of almond, olive or jojoba oil and wear it diluted.

Twinkle, Twinkle, Little Star

As I was writing this book I put a request up on my website for contributions from Teen Witches, which is how I met Jessica. She sent me an amazing email about her internet Teen Witch meeting place called NightStar Teen Pagan Network, which can be found at ww.nightmoon.org. au/nightstar/

Of course I wanted to meet her in person straight away and organised to have a coffee together. Little did I know the trouble she went to for what was to be a clandestine meeting, with her jumping every time her mobile phone rang – Jessica is one of many Teen Witches whose family unfortunately doesn't support their spiritual interests (in this case it's only her father, but his disapproval is intense). As I say in the chapter 'Parents – Can't Live With Them, Can't Live Without Them' it's always good to have the support of your parents . . . but sometimes it can be a hard thing to achieve!

This is very unfortunate because Jessica is utterly talented and motivated – and gorgeous – and a leading light in the growing world of Teen Witchcraft. We managed to get quite a lot discussed in our forty-eight minutes together before she had to jump in a cab and get back to where she was being picked up. Was she rebelling against her father's expectations? Yes, she was, but she is one of the most inspiring and delightful Witches, Teen or otherwise who I have met in a long time, and the time taken for this interview should prove valuable to every Teen Witch.

Jessica, what inspired you to set up a Teen Witch/ Pagan Network?

NightStar came about after a disturbing incident with my father. I had been starting to explore Witchcraft and one day he found out and trashed all my Witchy stuff. But probably the main inspiration would have to be the fact that there was nowhere for me to go in regards to following my Path. At the time I was fourteen and most established Pagan organisations refuse to be associated with anyone minor under the age of eighteen. I, and some other teenagers in similar situations as mine, needed a place where we could talk, gain knowledge and learn in an environment where no-one was going to ridicule us or throw derogatory comments our way.

How did you go about it?

Well, as I was a member of an organisation called NightMoon Pagan Network (now the sister-ship to NightStar for people over eighteen) and as the founder,

Adrian, and I are good friends, he told me that he would help me set it up. I wrote a letter to *Australian Witchcraft Magazine*, telling them of my plight and situation and asked for anyone else who would like to be involved in organising a place where we could talk and be supportive of each other. I had a great response with many well-wishings but no real assistance. So I searched the Net and chat rooms where I met Tim. Tim is my co-founder of the network and he helps to make sure it runs properly when I'm not around.

Adrian did all the web-weaving and crafted us a place like NightMoon but the only regulation to join was that you be under eighteen! I had to make all the basic rules of the network, such as equality to all members no matter what Path they follow, because not all of our members are Wiccan. With anything you need to be able to control things happening in and around the network because you don't want members being silly and using other members' personal information, such as email addresses, in an unsuitable way.

After that we started to add things to the site's Book of Shadows, as each member has their own page on the site. We set up an emailing list where members can talk and discuss anything of interest to them, mainly relating to the Craft. A discussion forum was also created, and we even made a section where there were some fun things like wallpaper for your computer's desktop and tarot and moon phase programs. We established a committee of people who were assigned specific duties such as media/relations officer and co-founders in order to operate the network smoothly. (Adrian helps watch over everything to make sure nothing goes wrong as we are associated with NightMoon.) After all this, all we had to do was wait for the member numbers to grow. And grow they have: in two years we now have over 800 members! It's fantastic to see that we are doing something that so many teens have a need for!

What service do you think your network best provides?

Our main aim was to provide a place where teens interested in the Craft could talk and discuss the things that really concerned them or just something that was on their minds. We provide a place that is free from any harassment of any sort where all members aged twelve to eighteen can learn from each other and be supportive. It's great for people to know that they are not alone out there in this world and what they are interested in is in no way wrong, bad or anything else that it may have been labelled. It's also great to know that there are other people your age who are going through a hard time finding and searching for their religious beliefs, and it feels so comforting to hear someone say 'I know what that feels like'. At NightStar the members are around for each other. When someone needs help everyone pitches in to help discover a solution and many people have made fantastic friends and even met up with them in real life. However, one of the best things that the network provides is a contact point, especially when you've been ostracised.

Are there any hidden dangers for Teen Witches on the Net?

With anything in today's world there are always dangers.

One of the things that we are really adamant about is giving out personal details to people, such as phone numbers and addresses. There is always a possibility that the person you have met is not truly who they say they are. Also, if the members do decide to meet up in person, we urge them to meet in a public place and take one or more people with them, just in case something unexpected happens. You just never know. Just as you wouldn't meet someone in the street and tell them your address and phone number after only talking to them for a minute, you wouldn't do it over the Net. Also, with many people trying to meet young people for all the wrong reasons (such as pornography), we ask the members if anything weird has been going on – such as requests for partners in sexual magic – to tell us. But the good thing is that members usually look out for each other in this way.

Jessica, tell me a little about yourself – what's school like and what interests and hobbies do you have?

Well, personally I have always gone to Catholic schools (shock horror!) and been brought up as a Catholic. I have grown up in Melbourne all my life. I'm interested in Wicca and Paganism of course, and your typical teenage girl things such as guys, clothes, music and hanging out with my girl-friends. I love soccer and horse-riding and I'm always reading, whether it be a book on Wicca or a novel! But don't get me wrong – I absolutely love going out to the movies or shopping or even clubbing with my friends. I don't want anyone to think that because I'm so involved in Witchcraft all I do is sit in a dark room doing spells: it's quite the opposite. I'm an outgoing and bubbly person who loves nothing more than being outside in the sun-shine close to nature!

Along with all this, I hold down three jobs while doing Year Twelve. So I'm a pretty busy person along with my Witchcraft, personal, school and family commitments.

Can you describe your parents' attitude to your interest in Wicca?

That would have to have been one of the hardest things I have had to face in my life. One time Dad came into my room while I was on the computer and saw some emails that I had received from a Witchcraft mailing list. He didn't give me a chance to explain and told me that I was a devil worshipper and that there was something wrong with me, and asked what I was learning at my Catholic school. Then he started to search my room. He delved into the drawer that I kept all my tools and workings in, and that was the final straw I guess … in the end everything was destroyed, including all my tools, spells and writings, along with my Book of Shadows. All I could say was that he may take away my material things but he could never steal from me my spirit. He searches my room regularly and often wisecracks about my Witchcraft. He thinks I don't do it anymore and I hate keeping it from him, but I think he's being unreasonable and hard on me about it. I don't impose my beliefs on other people, like some religions. I keep it to myself and go about it quietly. Wicca has helped me find myself in a way I didn't know existed and it makes me feel a part of something really unique and worthwhile. I guess it's just all these misconceptions that society has created, which stem from mainstream religion's negative attitude towards Witchcraft that cause the trouble.

My mother is fantastic. She sometimes gets a little apprehensive because she doesn't fully understand, but she supports me. I remember when Dad found out, she asked if something had happened to me in Church that made me turn away from 'God'. I simply told her that I didn't agree with the Catholic Church's teachings and restrictions, along with the many contradictions in the Bible. I feel that, because mainstream religion is forced down young people's throats from birth, it isn't always the right path for them to follow. In my case, I felt the Church was so ancient and set in its ways I just couldn't relate to or understand it. I don't like the fact that in the Church's teachings there's the one and only way. That's not the way life is. But don't get me wrong, history is great and you need it to form a foundation, but you also need to move with the times and changes.

What do your friends and schoolmates think of your interests?

Well, my close friends are absolutely fantastic! Another friend is also very supportive, because she too is interested

in Wicca. They are all genuinely interested and supportive. However, they don't like to ask too many questions or
to impose in any way. I guess I'm lucky that my friends are
like me in most ways. They don't like to be like everyone
else but they equally only follow what feels right for them.
Some of them think that it's pretty cool to have a best
friend who is a Witch while other people who aren't as
close to me think that it's either 'cool' or a load of bull.
But it doesn't bother me much because my energy is
wasted on them. However, if they start to say ridiculous
things, then I speak out and usually win! My boyfriends
have had a different approach. They like it to be proved to
them in a physical way! They seem to be intrigued by
having a girlfriend who is a Witch!

**Do you try to keep your interest fairly private (espe-
cially at school) or are you open about it all?**

I don't advertise it on a billboard or anything. If religion
is the topic of conversation and someone asks me, then I
will usually tell them what my beliefs are. However, if I
don't feel I can trust them or they are immature, I won't
say anything. I have, however, used my knowledge of
Witchcraft at school, like writing essays in English class.
But going to a private Catholic school, I don't exactly walk
around with a sign saying 'Hey, I'm a Witch!' Sometimes
you just have to be careful!

**How do your teachers react? Especially, for example,
when you write a piece on Wicca for your English
assignment? And how do you cope with compulsory Catholic religious training?**

I have found that some teachers whom I have submitted work to are genuinely interested in Witchcraft. A lot of them, believe it or not, think that it was an old wives' tale! They often ask me questions about what I do, with the most common question being: 'Does it really work?' When I submitted a piece on positive and negative magick for an English journalistic piece, my teacher said it was great to read something that was different – and he is also my religion teacher!

Religion, however, in its entirety is a different story. I have to grin and bear it almost. I have no say in what school I go to – my parents decided that Catholic is the best and in their opinion it provides me with the best opportunity for the future. I have no real problem with that. I've accepted that, as part of going to my school, I have to sit through the torturous compulsory religion classes. It's not that bad sometimes, but other times it is, especially when we were talking about a letter sent out by the Archbishop of Melbourne who said that the media was turning away young people from their faith. That was really hard for me to stomach – and I had to sit there and listen and not start a debate on the real reasons why the Church is losing followers! I usually tune out and just do other work or talk to my friends! When assignments come round, it's a bit harder but I manage.

Witchcraft is a demanding path – how do you cope with all your schoolwork, and your part-time jobs?

Sometimes it's extremely hard to manage! With three jobs, a Year Twelve workload, NightStar, family commitments and friends, it's just so hard to get everything done!

Sometimes I don't have time to do a full ritual on a special day, but I always make an effort to do something small like light a candle and chant in honour of the deities. I think one of the most important aspects is good old time management and prioritising. When something means enough to you and you are serious about it, you will always make some time for it!

What do you like best about being a Teen Witch?

The best thing is the freedom. You are not told to do everything at an exact time, and things are adaptable. Also, learning in a free environment and gaining knowledge that is so sacred and wonderful feels fantastic. Knowing you are also giving back to the Earth in some ways is fantastic as well. Also, having the power to make things happen for yourself and not waiting around for fate is tremendous.

However, Witchcraft is not in any way a means for getting whatever you need when you think you need it. In Witchcraft you have to be able to give as well as receive. As soon as you start asking and asking, you lose your connection with the Goddess and God – it's not worth the consequences.

It's not so much the teen aspect, but I guess that it is harder being so young because people don't take you seriously. I mean, I'm seventeen and still people think that I'm a ten-year-old playing fairy tales when I talk about Witchcraft sometimes.

What are the best and worst elements of the growing popularity of Teen Witchcraft and the way it's portrayed in popular media?

Media can be a great thing sometimes. Witchcraft is getting a fabulous amount of exposure and people are starting to realise that it is so much becoming a part of people's everyday lives and it's not devil worshipping! Teens are looking for something that does not force them to do things they do not want to, and they are searching for that feeling of belonging. And the media coverage makes getting information easier. However, with popular media such as TV shows like *Sabrina* and *Charmed*, you need to make sure that people know it's only entertainment value and you can not, no matter how much of a fantastic Witch you are, point your finger and get a boyfriend! Witchcraft is realistic! I think the media needs to start researching factual Witchcraft because I certainly don't go fighting demons every day after school! I love *Charmed* and can sometimes pick up some truth in what the girls do – however, we have to remember that the fight for television ratings is high and the truth just doesn't cut it as far as shock value sometimes.

It's great that Witchcraft is rapidly becoming more acceptable and accessible! Before everything was done in secret and hidden away. It's just so out there now! Now more and more teens are grasping the great things that Witchcraft can offer and their initial interest is often fuelled by the media. However, the people who are genuinely interested in it will stick with it for the long run, where those who are only dabblers will lose interest after a few months, because your spells don't work if you aren't sincere in your beliefs and intentions!

What's the most effective spell you've done?

To be honest, I don't actually do too many spells mainly

because I don't have a lot of time and I don't feel I should ask for everything that I want. Most of it will come to me in good time if it was meant for me – however, sometimes things do need that extra little push!

During one of last year's blue moons I did a ritual with a good friend of mine, and that was a first because I usually prefer to work solitary. We used both our energies to wish for things that we would like to be directed our way for the coming year. That was pretty successful. I received everything that I indicated I would like: I found out who my true friends were, I went very well at school, I met that special guy and my family relations started to improve. However, I wasn't very successful in deciding what to do with them when they came my way, so results like the guy didn't go exactly to plan. But that's another story!

Have you ever done any spells you now regret?

One time I wished to meet someone special who valued me for me and whom I could get along with. A terrific guy was sent to me and that was the problem – I was only sixteen and he was twenty-four. However, once he was sent to me I didn't use any magick to keep him! I left that up to the more natural forces of nature. To cut a long story short, I fell so deeply in love with him that when it came time to let him go I couldn't. I shared things with this person that I had never felt before. Sure, I am young and all but I know this was unique. Some people go their whole lives without ever finding anyone special. However, when this person met another person and they started going out I couldn't handle it. I did something selfish and I broke them up. It took three months to work but it did. I don't know what I planned to achieve but for some reason I had to do it. I feel bad that I did such a thing, but it was so important to me that I was willing to accept all karmic consequences of my actions and the threefold law. But believe me – I'm paying for it!

Do people approach you at school for spells and, if they do, what kind of spells do they ask for?

They sure do! The most common ones are to get great marks and to find a boyfriend or to get someone specific to fall in love with them. People seem to think that you can ask for anything and get it. Usually you can achieve what you want if you are sincere in your intentions. I don't like to do spells for people because it means that I am getting all the energy back if they are not exactly ethical. If I think the person is deserving of what they want, I may help them by telling them what they can do or writing up a ritual for them. But I'm not the world's most experienced Witch – I've only been practising for three years – and I have so much more to learn before I take other people's fate into my hands!

What's the nicest thing anyone's said to you about being a Teen Witch?

I think the nicest thing is just to be truly accepting of my beliefs and my choices. See, a lot of people don't think I can be a Witch because I don't dress like a Goth or act weird. I'm pretty normal I guess, if there's such a thing. I don't think anyone has ever said anything that can be deemed genuinely nice, although my friends always say nice things I guess. The nicest thing would probably be something as simple as a 'thank you' for help – answering this question has made me realise that not many people say nice things about me being a Witch!

What's the worst?

I think the worst would have to be accusing me of being a devil worshipper, a follower of Satan, an absolute mental nut case – that sort of stuff. It doesn't really bother me any more because I'm used to it, I guess, but I shouldn't have to put up with it. You learn to ignore all these sorts of comments, mainly because you know yourself they aren't true!

What do you think the difference is between a Teen Witch and an Adult Witch?

Well, it depends. Sometimes a Teen Witch can have more experience than an adult Witch if they have been practising for a longer period of time. However, an adult Witch usually has more maturity and can often practise without hindrance where most Teen Witches live with their parents, who sometimes don't approve, so it's hard! Adult Witches are usually more dedicated and have a deeper understanding of the Craft and its ways, because they have experienced more of life. However, some Teen Witches are so much like the adult Witches in their thoughts and actions because they, too, are here in this world and are going through things that change them. Some people grow up more quickly than others – you just have to be a little more patient with teens!

What sort of support do you think Witches should be giving Teen Witches?

I feel that adult Witches should be more tolerant and supportive of the younger members of the Craft. We are not all 'dabblers' and 'a bunch of immature teenyboppers' as I've heard it put before. They should try and help teach the ways of the Craft, because you don't want things to be distorted and you don't want teens turning away from their paths because they feel rejected! Younger Witches need the emotional support and they need to feel accepted because in reality they are the future of the Craft!

However, I feel that older Witches are getting much more used to the idea of having younger, true followers around, and most of them feel that having new followers is a great thing for the Craft. Older Witches are the only ones we can truly learn from.

Poetry, Spells, Insights and Art!

While I was writing *Life's A Witch!*, it occurred to me that the best way to find out how today's Teen Witches think was to invite them to contribute their insights, poems, drawings and their favourite spells to be published in this book. Here are the results!

Thank you! and Blessed Be.

✳ ✳ ✳

Lunar Dance
by Elissa ✳ Lithiafairy ✳ (age sixteen)

She treads the starfield of eternal night,
And spreads her powdery moonrays as she goes.
Her silvered aura is pure and light,
Her eyes laugh, her skin is translucent white,
she glows . . .

She carries her glowing orb as she walks,
To meet her equal, the Sun God.
She shakes her hands across the sky,
Covering the deep velvet she just laid,
With dusty trails of moondust, shining bright.
She twirls and dances to the silent moonsong,
She spirals and swirls all night long,
She guides me in my dreams and through my rites,
She is the lunar mother, of dreams and of night.

Lunar mother, growing in your spiral dance,
Waxing, waning, full and dark,
Spellbinding majick, settles in a trance,
Of blue, silver, moonrays and stars . . .

✳ ✳ ✳

Hecate's Rite

Hecate shrouds me in her dark veil,
Of mysteries, secrets, strength and love,
My darkness I've searched but to no avail,
My protection I wish to fall from above.

Hecate, my Goddess, hear my plight,
Through all darkness, I will be happy this night.
Drop your web and take the fear,
My troubles and woe will disappear,

Hecate, Kali, Lilith and all the crones,
Life, Death, Light and Dark,
Avail me now and end my fear . . .

✳ ✳ ✳

Ode to Artemis

Artemis flies her light across the sky,
Lighting the path of the unknown.
Glittering the sky with silvered sparkles,
And dusting the world below with blue powdered light.

She throws her orb across the velvet sky,
And it reaches me like a milky cloud.
Her power and majick entwines with mine,
To create a vortex of luminescent blue.

We propel the spell into the realms
And I feel the crescent light across my brow.
We whisper 'So mote it be . . . Our rite is done.'
And she flies back into the night . . .

* * *

Mountain View
by Jacqui

The grass is green,
The sky is blue,
And everything looks like
It's all brand new.
From the mountain we can see
All around from tree to tree,
We can see above and below
And we can see the river flow.
On the road we do go fast,
And everything we see goes into the past,
The trees are high,
The grass is low,
And when I see it,

My eyes glow.
I wish I could see it everyday,
But that's impossible,
There is no way.

✳ ✳ ✳

Untitled
by Jeffrey ✳ (age fourteen)

A thin spider thread ties my lips,
The candleflame lights her hips,
I hear the Goddess whisper in my ear,
The path of my journey is ever so clear.

Dark circles call to me,
They tell me they'll let me free,
The blade of my athame knows how to bite,
But the dark shadows trap me in the night.

I can't find the goddess in my heart,
I'm trapped in a portrait of Picasso's art,
Nothing is clear and the Goddess is gone,
I've been trying to escape since the day I was born.

Burn the books of the past,
I'll drink blood to make this last,
A web of my own lies has caught me,
And now I'm cutting it down so I can be free.

With the energy of my athame,
I can see the light of day,
And push these dark shadows away,
I know the God and Goddess are here to stay,

In my heart.

* * *

Miss Butterfly
by Chitra * (age sixteen)

Missy,
You're keeping a secret,
Holding it hidden,
Under your webbing.

Wanting to escape,
Run and not hide,
Fly and not fall,
Swim and not drown,
And find your way home.

The past seems like a dream,
A room filled with smoke,
The smell of disgust
Still lingers about.

What can you do,
To make the air fresh?
Look in your self,
The answer is there.

A Protection Spell
by Ella * (age eighteen)

Stand before any fire, look into the flames (or flame if you're using a candle), and visualise the fire bathing you with glowing, protective light. The fire creates a flaming, shimmering sphere around you. If you wish say, the following words:

Craft the spell in the fire;
Craft it well; weave it higher.
Weave it now of shining flame;
None shall come to hurt or maim.
None shall pass this fiery wall;
None shall pass, No, none at all.

Repeat when necessary.

Also, I have a Wishing Spell for you:

You will need three bay leaves. When the moon is new, write your wish out on paper. Visualise your wish coming true as you do so. Fold the paper into thirds and place three bay leaves inside the paper and visualise your wish coming true. Fold the paper into thirds again and hide it in a dark place. Keep visualising your wish coming true as you do this.

When it comes true burn the paper as an offering.

Memory spell – for finding lost things
by Slayerbabe 182

Dear Fiona – I have a spell which worked for me, and it should help everyone else, too.

Before going to sleep, take a bowl of fresh water and any small crystal into your bedroom. Sit with the water in front of you and the crystal in your hand and visualise the last place you saw the lost item.

Place the crystal in the bowl and place under your bed, then breathe calmly and say:

Spirits of the east and west,
Guide me in the realm of dreams,
Take me to a place of visions
And lead me to what has been lost.

Go to sleep. In the morning take the crystal out of the water and carry it with you throughout the day to help you jog your memory.

$$* \quad * \quad *$$

Spells and Legends
by Miss Chicky

Hey Fiona, I have a little spell for your new book:

If your hairclip's come loose it means that someone you love is thinking about you.

If the clip comes out, take it and whisper your beloved's name three times. If you haven't seen them in a while and want them to get in touch, imagine their face and see yourself playing with their hair and lightly kissing their brow.

Put the clip back in your hair and you'll hear from them soon.

Here are some legends:

If you have the hiccups, it means someone you love misses you. Take a deep breath and say '(his/her name), I miss you too.' If it's the right person who is missing you, your hiccups will be gone!

If the clasp on your necklace falls to the front of your neck, someone you love is thinking of you. Take the clasp and kiss it, whispering their name and maybe a special message or wish, and place it behind your neck as usual. They will get your message.

If the left ear is burning, someone is speaking nicely or lovingly of you. If the right is burning, then nasty words of you are being spoken.

If your palms are itchy, it means good luck. The same if a spider is in your home, or a bird poops on you.

These are off the top of my head:

Roses are red, pure and true,
Here is a message just for you:
When you're alone think of me only
'Cause with me by your side
You'll never be lonely.

I'm lost in a world, I'm lost in his eyes,
I'm lost in his smile, I'm lost without lies,
I'm lost in love.

True friends are like diamonds, precious and rare,
False ones are like Autumn leaves found everywhere.

Depression is merely anger without enthusiasm.

✳ ✳ ✳

Healing spell for a Loved One in Pain

by Kym ✳ (age seventeen)

Hi! I made up a really simple healing spell for my mother which was very effective. It is as follows:

Sit comfortably in a place where you won't be disturbed and meditate for a few minutes to clear your mind. Start to focus on the person you want to heal and the pain you want to stop. It could be physical or emotional. I did this when my mum sprained her ankle so it was physical.

When you have a clear picture of the person and their pain, bring your arms out in front of you and slowly start to circle the palms of your hand around each other, like you're rolling an invisible ball. As you do this, envision a ball of bright blue light start to form between your hands. Keep doing this and thinking about your loved one until the ball is large and bright in your hands and you can almost feel it. Then, throw your hands up in the air, throwing the ball of blue light to the person. See it surround them and settle on the site of their pain and gently start to be absorbed and heal the pain. When the light begins to fade from your vision, the spell should be working on them.

You have a choice about what you do after this. I went to bed and didn't tell anyone about it until I spoke to my mum again, which was about a week as she was on holidays. She said she was better the second day she was away, which was the day after I did this spell.

✳ ✳ ✳

Dear Fiona,
I have been into witchcraft for about two years. I am twelve, thirteen in three months. I have been writing some spells and I'd love to know what you think of them.
from Jessica

Beauty Spell

Beautiful in and
Beautiful out,
May I never be without.
Place all the glamour upon me
With shining hair,
Red rosy lips,
Perfect legs and
The right sized tits.
May I be nice and kind
And my presence be seen by even the blind,
May I glow with love and kindness
Radiant in my blindness.
May I be loved for who I am not what I wear and with

who I hang,
Beautiful in and
Beautiful out,
May I never be without.

✳ ✳ ✳

Provoke Water Power

Water power come to me,
I need the power to set me free.
Balance the light with the dark,
Leave me with no obvious mark.
I provoke the power buried deep inside,
May it never ever hide.
May the power be good and pure,
And of demons there shall be fewer.
Water I am yours,
Please open the doors.
Water you are mine,
This is a declaration to the divine.
Enter me so I can be
Flowing water is where I find peace.
Rough or calm,
Quiet or loud,
Water is my every thing.
So Mote It Be.

✳ ✳ ✳

Travel Protection

Angels of the sky,
Spirits of the wind,
Protect me on my journey to other lands,

Guide me with your gentle hands.
I place my trust in you, please say you'll be true.
It's you I trust,
It's you I need,
While I'm flying overseas.
So Mote It Be.

✳ ✳ ✳

Rain Spell

Spirits' tears pierce the sky,
Spirits' tears cry, cry.
Open the skies to let rain through,
Clouds open, please do.
Rain fall and wetness go,
Rain fall flow, flow.
Think of the streams empty and low,
Think of the people who want water to flow.
Spirits' tears pierce the sky
Spirits' tears cry, cry.

✳ ✳ ✳

A Prayer to the Great Life Spirit
by Caitlin ✳ (age thirteen)

I'm a practising witch (with my mum). I would like to contribute the prayer that I read at my grandmother's funeral in January this year. It comes from a passage in one of the books in the series 'The Witches of Eileanan' by Kate Forsyth. My mum and I found it really moving and very appropriate for a chant or blessing at anytime.

Ea, ever-changing life and death,
transform us in your sight, open your
secrets, open the door. In you we shall
be free of darkness without light, and
in you we shall be free of light
without darkness. For both shadow
and radiance are yours, as both life
and death are yours. For you are the
rocks and trees and stars and the
deep, deep swell of the sea, you are the
spinner and the weaver and the cutter
of the thread, you are birth and life
and death, you are shadow and
brightness, you are night and day,
dusk and dawn, you are ever-changing
life and death.

Blessed be !

* * *

A Letter
from Lidz * (age eighteen)

Dear Fiona,
It's true that the world would be a dreary place without
personal beliefs! I currently study at university and have
spent a lot of time in the past year or so discovering my
witchy half.

The point I would like to make is this: witchiness is
present everywhere, even in my study of straight and sensible, and I think it's fantastic that people like yourself are
able to come out and tell the world that these ideas are
perfectly natural, especially us teenagers (who, let's face it,

can be scared about all!). It is important to know that there are people who live very ordinary witchy lives rather than the stereotypical picture.

Also, many things such as the Gaia theory are very acceptable at university, and for those who don't know I would remind them that these kinds of things can be studied. It's not all maths and physics! I guess what I'm trying to say is that there is no need to choose between something like Uni and witchiness – they can coexist.

No-one told me that and I think it would really have helped me.

✷ ✷ ✷

To Me From Me
by Fiona Horne ✷ (age seventeen)

Here's a final insight from a little girl I once knew! This is something I wrote when I was seventeen in my first Book of Shadows – though I didn't call it that at the time. It was just a notebook, but I can see now it was the start of something big!

> *Reading about the Craft is a valid pursuit and use of time, because as I read, it exists in my mind. This is just as valid as a physical ritual to express and reaffirm my beliefs.*
>
> *A healthy body will make me a more efficient Witch!*
>
> *Adults use ten per cent of our brains – the key to the other ninety per cent is myth and ritual. When a child is born I think they use one hundred per cent of their brain before becoming adult-erated. Imagination, games, ritual and 'make believe' are the keys to opening up to magickal powers and the other ninety per cent of our brains.*
>
> *The key to practising the Craft (which I feel instinctively is*

*my heritage) is meditation – stilling and focusing my mind.
When I am feeling unconfident in ritual, all I need to do is
stop and meditate. If I take it slow I will eventually evolve as
I'm meant to – 'You are on the Path, you don't need to know
where it goes, just follow it'. One small step at a time will
gradually integrate the Craft into my everyday life.*

*Magick and beliefs aren't about how many rituals you do,
how complicated they are, or if you did them correctly. It's about
feeling it deep inside and integrating it plus connecting with
the timeless knowledge of ourselves that we are born with and
forget as we 'grow up'. Just do what feels right, relax and there
will be time for everything. Belief in yourself and your methods
is all you need.*

✳ ✳ ✳

My Goddess
by Jackie ✳ (age seventeen)

The smile that spreads across my face with all the
Warmth and potency of the sun is induced by her.
All of the passion and intensity that burst from my heart.
That unique shimmer in my eyes.
They're all because of her.
The maiden, the mother, the crone.
She is my love, my light, my peace, my simplicity, destiny.
My one protector who is here with me for all of time.
I am the radiant woman I am because of her.
She is the Goddess. My Goddess.

* * *

Enchantress – Magick Weaver
by Stephanie (aka Aldora Nightfire)

This drawing was inspired by the immense power and energy that can be created through mind, body and spirit. The power, force and essence of Magick.

* * *

A Magickal Dream on the Eve of the Winter Solstice
by Katie

Top Teen Witch Tips

WHAT TO WEAR?

Some of you may have heard the term 'skyclad' and if you're wondering what it means it's 'clad by the sky' or in other words 'naked'! As Witches, we accept our bodies as perfect and sacred and it's often appropriate to do our rituals and spells with nothing between us and the sky. Most solitary Witches work that way at least some of the time, and among Covens and other groups you'll find that some work robed (or otherwise clothed), some work skyclad, and some just go with letting people make up their own mind about how they feel on the night. Having said that, you don't have to work skyclad to be an effective Witch and if anyone ever tries to force you to get your gear off for ritual, don't stick around! An all-skyclad group might only accept people who are cool about the idea, which is fair enough. If you're not happy working that way though, just start looking elsewhere. While the Craft teaches that 'Naked is Sacred', no Witch worth her or his salt (or water or oil or incense!) would ever think they were helping anyone by forcing them to do something against their own judgement.

If you're under eighteen this is all sort of in the abstract anyway, since most Covens don't accept members under that age. As Teen Witches, you'd probably want to wear something if you're working in a little group anyway and maybe consider going skyclad just for solitary Circles or for when you hit the adult years.

I have a couple of special garments that I save for Witchy work (sometimes it's just too cold for skyclad work!). Teen Witches don't need elaborate robes (though you can have them if you want). You also don't have to own a pentagram necklace either (though heaps of Teen Witches do). Try to keep one special outfit that you wear only for your Witchy stuff. What's important in all this is that you feel sacred and special when you're practising Witchcraft – inside and out.

A tip: If you are wearing regular gear and want to purify it for ritual, trace a pentagram of incense (sandalwood or frankincense blends are good) and walk through it (wearing the gear you want to purify).

SOMETHING SIMPLE

Here's a ritual you can start and end the day with to remind yourself that you are a Teen Witch.

Stand somewhere where there is nothing between the top of your head and the sky. By this I mean it's preferable that you stand outside, but if you can't, stick your head out the window!

Breathe in deeply and think for a minute what it means to you to be a Teen Witch – you may focus on the sense of empowerment and peace it gives you or the fun you have casting spells. Every time you do this you may focus on a different aspect. When you are ready, in your mind's eye see your crown chakra (the energy centre at the top of your head) open up and a stream of white light pour out into the sky. This is your offering to the Universe, and in doing this you are sharing your positive power with all things. When you are ready, focus on the light pouring back into you – now equally charged by positive energies around you. As it pours in, focus again on your commitment to being the best you can be and a powerful Teen Witch. When you are overflowing with white light, make the sign of the pentagram by touching first your third eye, then your right nipple, left shoulder, right shoulder, left nipple and then third eye again.

The ritual is complete!

KEEPING ON TRACK

Sometimes there seems to be so much to remember – so many rituals to do, so many sabbats and esbats to celebrate – that you're having a hard enough time keeping up with your schoolwork; that you feel like chucking it all in and giving up on exploring the Craft. Hold on! Don't panic. Many, many times in the first few years I felt that the more I knew, the more I didn't know and I would get stressed out. Always try to keep in your mind that it's 100 percent OK to take all the time you need in this very developmental stage of your Craft, but try to keep connected by doing something rather than giving everything up. Even if this means just reading a Crafty novel by an author like Australian Kate Forsyth (her 'Witches of Eileanan' series is amazingly inspiring and a great read!).

Stay in touch with your inner Witchiness (picture it bubbling away like a cauldron inside you) and no doubt you'll be drawn to more formal practice again a little further down the track. Witchcraft is not about making your life harder, it's about making it easier and more enjoyable — so if it doesn't feel like it's flowing, just sit tight until it does again.

WHY AREN'T MY SPELLS WORKING?

If your spells aren't working, are you doing the right spells? Are you clear on your intent, obeying the Witches' Laws and not being manipulative? Sometimes spells will backfire or just not work if you are trying to interfere with others' free will, or if you are working from a selfish perspective. (One thing the *Charmed* sisters get right in TV land is that they are to use their powers to help and protect the innocent — not for their own gain.) Remember, too, that some spells do need to be repeated to get the job done. If you're cutting wood with an axe, you often need to give a log a lot more than one single whack. Spells work just the same way. Sometimes you hit the jackpot first time round; other times you need to keep on repeating the out-pouring of energy in order to cut through obstacles. Just don't repeat the spell too often. Give it time to work. For a major goal in your life, casting the spell once or maybe twice max in a lunar month (on a new moon and full moon) is the most you should be doing. Other spells, like healings, seem to respond to a slow, steady outpouring of magic, like burning a candle for someone each night till improvement is felt.

However, if you are sure that your purpose is honest and pure and your spells still aren't hitting their mark, go through this check list:

Having a Magickal Plan

1. Have a clear idea of what you're doing and what result you're hoping to achieve.
2. What are the likely outcomes? That is, how is it going to affect others, not only yourself?
3. Make sure you memorise your incantations and invocations well before you do the spell so that you don't have to keep referring back to a book, which will break your concentration and interfere with the powers you are conjuring.
4. When you are spellcasting remember to take your time, breathe and concentrate on your visualisation skills. Don't rush it! Focus and let the powers swirl around inside and outside you, fuelling your intent.
5. Remember to take action not only on the mag-ickal, metaphysical plane, but also the physical. For example, if you cast a spell to go well in your

exams, you have to study too! The spell will help make your goals easier to achieve.

DREAM DIARY

In addition to your Book of Shadows you may like to keep a dream diary. Some of my best spells and ritual ideas have come from my dreams, and as you get into the habit of writing down your dreams, recalling them becomes easier.

Drinking a cup of mugwort tea before bed will help you more actively experience vivid dreams. If your schedule is so hectic that writing your dreams down every morning would take up too much time and stress you out, perhaps choose one night a week to go on a 'magickal dream flight'. Anoint a silver candle with some lavender oil and meditate on the flame as you drink your tea and mentally prepare for your night's journey.

I have had some pretty intense dreams when doing this. Once I dreamt I was in the kitchen of a country cottage with three other women. We were dressed in long, coarse linen skirts and had white caps over our hair. It was early in the evening and we were making a cake together. We were related – mother, aunt, grandmother and myself – and we were Witches. The cake we were making was an enchantment cake and whoever ate the first piece would become my husband. Together with four wooden ladles we stirred the eggs, corn flour, honey, caraway seeds, milk and crushed rose petals. Five drops of my blood was added (pricked from my thumb) and the four of us chanted a mumbled charm which I couldn't really understand as it seemed to be in another language.

Then the dream jumped ahead and it was night time.

The fire was glowing and the cake was on the table laid out on a piece of white cloth with a large knife next to it. Then three men entered the kitchen together. They were brothers and one of them was to be wed to me. I was aware that the magickal cake would help me choose the right one. Whoever was attracted to cut and eat the cake first would be my husband.

On waking I checked out the magickal properties of the cake ingredients and my dream was spot on! They were all traditional ingredients used in love and enchantment spells.

CREATING MAGICK

An important part of being a Teen Witch is being creative – expressing your inner self through art. It could be through music (the voice of the soul), playing an instrument and/or singing, painting, photography, writing or even coming up with complex and beautiful mathematical formulae! Be aware that life is never boring for a Teen Witch. There is always something to do that taps into and expands magickal potential within and without. So if everyone has a date on Saturday night except you, rather than sitting at home being bored and depressed, do something creative – decorate your Book of Shadows, write a song or do some Witchy research and create some spells. Throwing your hands up in the air and saying 'life sucks' is not an option for a Teen Witch!

CHALLENGE YOURSELF

Part of being a Teen Witch is challenging yourself mentally, spiritually and physically. Don't be afraid to be different and seek out challenges that push your further. Set yourself difficult tasks knowing that you have the desire and drive and magick to achieve them. So whether it's taking that extra subject, trying sky diving, or deciding that you want to be a movie star – just go for it! Use your Witchcraft to help you get there and to make you stronger, but remember to focus on and enjoy the journey, not just arriving at the destination.

BE QUIET!

Remember one of the Four Magickal Principles is 'To Be Silent'. If you are working spells, especially on yourself, don't tell anyone about it. Keep it quiet – that way you won't feel answerable to others' opinions of how your progress is going. Sometimes if people know you've got problems, their well-meaning concern or energy could just add fuel to your problem. Of course, if it's a situation like abuse or something that you know you shouldn't stay quiet about then you absolutely need to speak out and tell someone, but a lot of normal 'growing up' problems can be dealt with efficiently without attracting a lot of attention.

BE REALISTIC

Measure your successes on your own terms and don't compare your achievements or magickal advancements to others. As the *Desiderata* – a wonderfully insightful piece of writing – says: 'There will always be people greater and lesser than yourself.' So tread your Path confidently and righteously, forging your own journey.

During the writing of this book I caught part of a television documentary on an extraordinary man who passed away 1996. Sir Laurens Van der Post was a white man born in 1906 in South Africa. For many years he lived among the stone age Kalahari bushmen, one of the oldest cultures on Earth. He dedicated much of his life to teaching the West the importance of valuing the meaning and existence of indigenous cultures in the modern world. Even sixty years ago he was aware that the modern world was in danger of losing its spiritual identity to technology, racial and religious prejudice, empty consumerist values and a lack of understanding of the interconnectedness of all life. Van der Post wrote twenty-three books and was an utterly fascinating man (check out all the websites on him!). The television special featured an interview with him just before he died and one thing he said struck me as particularly profound. He was talking about his time with the Kalahari bushmen who live a very physically demanding and harsh life (especially compared to the creature comforts and support systems of the West). One of the major insights he experienced was this: for an individual to have a sense of *meaning* and purpose in life is ultimate. When you have meaning it doesn't matter whether you're happy or not – you are at one with spirit. This struck me as particularly relevant for Witches, teens or otherwise. No matter how difficult life gets, how worn out emotionally and physically I feel, I know that there is a purpose and meaning to my life and that I am not a random accident. As a Witch I continually explore my relationship with the world through rituals, spells, and just *being* a Witch, enjoying the outlook and perspective on life that being a Witch gives me.

JUST A THOUGHT!

One thing I have realised about modern Witchcraft is that, despite the huge amount of information about the traditional and right way to go about things, often the most meaningful and rewarding experiences come in those moments of absolute inspiration which follow any method or pre-ordained procedure. The experience might be coloured by your knowledge of these but it is not dictated by them.

This is an insight into the flexibility of Witchcraft – it's often the feeling and connection that matters most, not the procedure. For all the potential differences that this amount of flexibility allows, we have enough similarities to be considered unified. Our similarities are that we worship nature and recognise the Goddess and God within and without (although how we conceptualise them might vary from Witch to Witch). We also work magick: the art of changing consciousness and manifesting different realities at will.

There are wonderful new insights being reported on all the time in our Craft. We are a growing, evolving phenomenon. Some Witches like to look to our nebulous past for guidance, others prefer to live in it – but ultimately our greatest strength will be in our ability to evolve into the future and this is where the role of the Teen Witch lies.

ANOTHER THOUGHT

The world answers according to the questions you ask of it, and if you change the way you think, you'll be surprised what happens around you in response to these changes.

It's hard to accept this sometimes (even for Teen Witches with relatively short pasts and long futures) because humans hang onto the predictability of what we know from the past. In turbulent teen times we are especially just trying to stay afloat at the best of times, and hang onto the life raft of what we think we know.

However, part of being a Teen Witch is knowing that one of the most empowering things you can do is to accept responsibility for your thoughts, feelings and your reactions to others and events. Teen Witches need to look inside before they make a decision about the outside world, because usually the outside world will only be a problem when there is a problem within.

THE DAY AFTER

In the last stages of writing this book I got a major computer virus and all the files on my laptop seemed to be history. With the help of a technician I was able to go in quickly and save the work I'd done onto a floppy disk – however, at the time there was no guarantee that the files were not corrupted. I was in a remote country location and I could not get to another computer to see if my book had been saved. So for a while there I thought I'd lost all my work and would have to start writing my book again from scratch – which was utterly devastating. (Yes, I was stupid and hadn't backed up any of my files! Major magickal lesson there: always have a second string to your bow.)

Eventually, I found that the files were safe and I had not lost the book, but my laptop was inoperable and it was going to have to be pen and paper for the next few days until I could get onto a computer again. The following is what I wrote upon awakening the day after one of the worst days in my life.

Well, it's the day after the annihilation of my laptop. All night I had nightmares about the long, difficult day. But guess what? The sun is shining this morning and there is steam coming off the lavender bushes which line the front porch. I am warm, pen in hand, enjoying a cup of coffee and the fresh winter's morning air. If I had the laptop I wouldn't be doing this. I would be inside hunched over the table, manically pounding out words. Instead I sit, contemplating and watching low fluffy clouds scud across the top of the mountain, serenaded by the songs of different birds, and as I write I am enjoying watching the sharp shadow of my pen as it flits across the page. What happened yesterday was probably the worst thing possible, given my situation – killer deadlines and pressing television and radio commitments. But I've survived and in the wake of the turmoil of yesterday I feel calm and in some ways cleansed. Once again it's been proved that in the face of real adversity we find our greatest strengths. It is the Witch in me that helps me accept and understand what happened and the cyclical nature of it. Some of the trees around me are in the barren throes of winter, their gnarled branches stripped of leaves forming a latticework of crone energy against the blue sky. But on this cold, crisp day already I can see little green buds forming on the spidery twigs – everything renews itself, the sun always rises . . . at the end is another beginning.

Last night a friend told me a very sad story of a seventeen-year-old guy who was in Year 12 and under a lot of pressure to do well in his exams. His computer crashed big time and he lost his CAT essay – it was forty per cent of his mark, a major assessment. It wasn't backed up – it was gone. However, he didn't speak to his teachers, his parents or his friends. He felt so panicked and so isolated that he couldn't cope and he killed himself. This terribly tragic situation is unfortunately not an isolated event. There is so much pressure on teens and often the technology that is supposed to ease the situation sometimes only increases it.

A Teen Witch needs to fully comprehend the cyclical nature of life – things come and go and come again; begin, end and begin again. It's a necessary part of life's journey and we see it played out over and over again around us: in the blooming and withering of flowers, in the ebb and flow of the sea. Sometimes though, it can all just seem too much and this is where your Witchcraft can help. Last night before I knew the files were safe, I was so distraught I went into brain meltdown – I just sat staring at the wall thinking 'Oh no, oh no, oh no . . .'

I felt as if I was being sucked into a black hole and my life was just one big joke. I knew I had to do something, so I lit a charcoal disc and sprinkled a special 'inspiring and passionate' blend of incense on it – dragon's blood powder, cinnamon and myrhh. I whisked the smoke around with a blue feather that a rosella had kindly left in my path a couple of days before. I chanted Goddess names, 'Isis, Astarte, Diana, Hecate, Demeter, Kali, Inanna' and focused on releasing my problems and disappointments and allowing new healing energies and a sense of acceptance to breeze in.

I quickly started feeling much better and much more

prepared to move on and deal with the situation constructively and effectively.

The following is a vision quest ritual you can do to help cope when everything seems too much. It might be school, your parents, your friends, your siblings or just everything. It will help refresh you and cleanse your soul and give you rational insights into your current situation, so that you can move on positively and with a fully-charged heart.

CLEAR VISION RITUAL

Best time: whenever you need it!

You will need:

* A pale blue candle.
* Clary sage oil – this is about $20 a bottle but it's a wonderful investment as it is the best euphoric oil and has many uses. If you can't afford it, lavender can be substituted. You could also consider a blended oil – the 'Wise Woman' blend by Jurlique is divine and great for boys and girls as it captures the essence of the Goddess. (In this spell, it is one of her forms you will be invoking.)
* An aromatherapy oil burner.
* A feather.
* A piece of fabric that is brand new and large enough to wrap around you – gold cloth would be perfect, or perhaps a beautiful sarong. If you can't make anything new, just make sure that it has been washed and ironed.
* Peppermint tea.
* Honey.
* A sharp pin.

Cast Circle with the full ritual. Carve your name into the candle with the pin and trace the pentagram next to it. As

you do this, focus on how much you love your Witchcraft –
how it helps give you a sense of meaning and how it puts
you in touch with the beauty and bounty of life. In your
sacred Circle things are always beautiful and well no matter
what kind of turmoil is raging outside.

Lick your thumb and trace over your carving. Light the oil
burner, and on top of the water disperse seven drops of the
oil. When it starts to vaporise use the feather to waft the
scent towards you, inhaling deeply. When you are ready,
invoke the Goddess Rhiannon by draping your shoulders with
the cloth and saying:

Rhiannon, come visit me
On your white and glorious steed,
Help ease my woes and carry me
To a space where I can rest easy.

In your mind's eye, see Rhiannon ride into your Circle on her
beautiful white horse. She will invite you to join her, so
mount the horse with her and let her take you on a journey.
Notice where you are going, look at the scenery, the people,
the signs; listen to the sounds and smell the scents of your
journey. Try to remember everything and anything she may
say to you – all these will help your situation.

When you finally ride back into Circle and dismount thank
Rhiannon by saying:

Rhiannon of the day and night,
Thank you for this glorious flight
And journey into dark and light;
I am now blessed with great insight.

Immediately write down everything in your Book of Shadows
before you remove your cloak. Don't try to analyse anything,
just jot it all down.

When you have finished, drink some of the peppermint
tea with honey to refresh and centre yourself and eat a little

food as you normally would as part of your Circle ceremony.

In the next few days read over the notes you made and start to analyse and understand the wisdom there and how it can help you.

Note: You can use your cloak to connect with Rhiannon again, and if you had any trouble 'seeing' things clearly, you will find holding an amethyst crystal as you journey will assist your inner vision.

Magickal Meanings

Following are all the different ingredients, objects, colours and phases of the moon and sun for spells and rituals mentioned in this book. Before you do a spell or ritual it's important that you refer to this section so that you have a good understanding of why and what you're doing!

Just about all the ingredients mentioned are easily obtainable (check out the suppliers section). Also here's a suggestion: if you are ever curious as to what various herbs or trees look like in their natural growing state and don't know where to find them, go exploring in your local Botanical Garden. When I was first starting out on the Path, I would spend every weekend in the Sydney Botanical Gardens familiarising myself with various plants, trees and herbs – it's a gorgeous way to spend an afternoon and also helps improve your Witchcraft. Why not take a few fellow Teen Witches and a picnic lunch and make a day of it?

HERBS, FRUITS AND WOODS

Almond: Good for prosperity and promoting opulence and fertility of ideas and dreams. A wand made from almond wood is very good for a Teen Witch as it works to boost growing skills.

Apple: For good luck, wisdom and love (this fruit is considered sacred to the Greek Goddess of Love, Aphrodite). When the apple is cut across to expose the pentacle arrangement of the seeds, it is sacred for the celebration of Samhain or Halloween as it becomes a representation of the bridge of existence between life and death.

Bay leaves: Can be used to attract love and can imbue an object or written desire with magickal potency and the ability to manifest. They can also be used to inspire truth and confidence in the spoken word.

Berries: Strawberry, blackberry, cranberry, etc., all represent fertility, positivity and potency.

Black pepper: Can work to speed things up and bring ideas and plans to quicker fruition. Can also dispel negativity.

Borage blossom: Encourages a strong and passionate sense of self and the ability to feel joy and love even in the most demanding of circumstances.

Celery seed: Helps with concentration and can improve visualisation skills.

Chamomile: Healing, peace and love. Leave out in the sun to empower before a working. In ancient Egypt chamomile was dedicated to the Sun god for its curing powers.

Cinnamon: Can help to increase focus and mental powers, and it's also a bit of an aphrodisiac for the boys!

Can also bring good luck and fill a space with peaceful, content energy.

Cloves: For the ability to compel others to accept your will.

Corn flour: Good as a base for magickal powders.

Cucumber: Not only good for puffy eyes but can put you in touch with the subconscious and the wisdom we can reach through our intuition.

Dill seed: To make yourself irresistible!

Dragon's blood powder: This is not really powdered blood of dragon (they're an endangered species after all!) but the resin of a tree. It's great to power up love spells or indeed any ritual energy.

Frankincense: One of the most essential ingredients of magick: it's empowering, purifying, increases concentration, protective, and helps to bridge the spiritual and the everyday.

Garlic: One of the most purifying substances and very protective against negative energy, as well as being effective in completely banishing unwanted influences and presences.

Heart's ease (a type of violet): Promotes love and a full, happy heart.

Hops: Encourages restful sleep, and when burnt can cleanse a ritual space of unwanted energy

Ivy: For virtue and honesty.

Jasmine: Great for girls as it is the essence of the sacred feminine aspect of the Universe – use it to honour the Full Moon. It's also excellent for promoting psychic ability.

Lavender: One of my favourites and an all round staple for a magickal pantry. Increases magickal awareness, peace, is great for blessing, purifying, empowering, and can replace just about any other ingredient because of its incredibly pure vibrational qualities.

Lemon: For love and purification. Also good for focusing the intellect and to help with making choices.

Mugwort: One of the best Witchy herbs! Useful for protection (especially when travelling either in this world or between in dreams and meditations!). Also great for the consecration of Witches' tools (burn mugwort and pass the object through the smoke) and a general power booster, especially when doing rituals around the Full Moon.

Nutmeg: Good for enhancing psychic ability and encouraging effective meditations.

Oak leaves: To the Druids (whose practices are a major inspiration to modern Wicca) the oak tree is one of the most sacred trees – using any part of the tree, whether it be the leaves or bark (dried and powdered as incense), emphasises and magnifies Witchy energy!

Orange blossom: For love.

Orris root: For physical and spiritual protection and to promote love, honour, fidelity and companionship.

Parsley: Use to honour the Goddess in her Full Moon and maternal aspect, as it helps to invoke her presence.

Patchouli: An aphrodisiac which honours the Male and Female creative forces and the cycles of life. It is also used to invoke the Greek Goddess Hecate.

Peppermint: Can speed up bringing things to fruition and can also encourage more colourful and lucid dreams and divination.

Rose petals: For love, purity, friendship and protection.

Rosemary: Stabilises and strengthens, and can help increase memory, whether burnt as incense or essential oil or drunk as a tea. Rosemary is sacred to the dead and can be used to honour them. It is also good for protection and to purify spaces.

Rue: Protection, benevolence and to release the past.

Sage: Purification, healing and cleansing, strength, mental health, wisdom and banishing any evil.

Sandalwood: To do work with confidence and ease.

Senna pods: Promotes compassion and a willingness to cooperate.

St John's Wort: For high powered protection.

Strawberry: For fun, light heartedness and romance.

Tarragon: For calmness and compassion, and to bond with the feminine aspect of the universe.

Tea: For clarity and strength.

Thyme: Removes negativity and is great for spring cleaning and bringing in new energies.

Vervain (also called Verbena): Improves psychic ability and can also increase confidence and a sense of inner well being, especially when performing or doing the arts. It's great for protection and for love.

Willow: To move from one life to another, honouring another and protection.

Yarrow: Love and commitment.

ESSENTIAL OILS

Almond oil: Fertility of thoughts and ideas.

Cinnamon oil: Good to balance masculine energies, a stimulant and also promotes a sense of inner peace and wellbeing.

Frankincense oil: Purifying and protective.

Lemon oil: Nurturing, and honours the Lunar Essence.

Lavender oil: Healing, anti-depressive, great all round magickal energy.

Neroli: Balances feminine energies, minimises anxiety and promotes peace.

Olive oil: Good for consecration (blessing) of objects, this oil was sacred to the ancient Greeks and used for their sacred temple lamps.

Rose geranium: Calming, healing and loving.

Rosemary oil: Protective, enhances mental powers like memory.

Sunflower oil: Brings happiness and can also be used to bless objects. Honours the Solar Essence.

Ylang ylang: Soothing, sensual, disperses frustrations and promotes confidence.

THE CELESTIAL BODIES

THE MOON

The different phases of the moon can influence spell-casting and ritual.

Waxing: A good time to do spells for abundance and to manifest new dreams, goals and desires. Energy is building and a forward propulsion is manifest.

Full: Energy is peaking and this is a good time to do spells of all sorts, as well as honouring and worshipping the Goddess and giving thanks for being alive.

Waning: A time for banishing unwanted energies or presences, and also a time to get rid of bad habits and to bind unpleasant influences.

Dark: A good time for introspective work like divination or just to take a rest from magick all together!

THE SUN

Dawn: New beginnings, new goals, new dreams, and also a time to re-state intentions and recharge spells. If you have an amulet or talisman, leave it in the light of the dawning sun to recharge its potency.

Noon: A mega-potent time for charging up a spell, amulet or talisman, and also a great time for spells of abundance and empowerment, and to give thanks for all the good and meaningful things in life.

Dusk: A good time for spells of closure and release, and also for moving on, establishing new patterns and ideas.

COLOURS

Black: Banishing, binding and can be used to access the subconscious.

Blue: Healing and happiness.

Dark blue: Presence of mind.

Gold: Sun energy, empowerment and positivity.

Green: Prosperity, employment, fertility, successful use of efforts and skill.

Orange: Legal matters, also sun energy and pride.

Pale blue: Calming.

Pink: Love, self-confidence, luck.

Purple: Power, success, enhancement of psychic powers.

Red: Love, willpower, courage, ambition.

Silver: Represents the Goddess and lunar energy, as well as purity, and can stimulate the intuition.

White: Can replace any other colour (except black), and represents purity and protection.

Yellow: Wisdom, stimulates the intellect, and aids concentration.

CANDLE MAGICK

Among the easiest and most effective spells are those which are conjured by candle magick. The elements of fire and air come into play to encourage quick and effective results. Choose a coloured candle corresponding to your desire or goal.

With a pin or knife, carve in words or symbols of your desire or goal, and then underneath carve the Witches' Pentagram (the five pointed star). Lick your thumb and trace over your carvings to seal your energy into the spell. To charge up the spell, either with your spit or an essential oil relative to your needs, anoint the pentagram you've carved into the candle with your thumb. Trace either widdershins (clockwise in the Southern Hemisphere, or against the sun) to take something away, or deosil (anti-clockwise in the Southern Hemisphere or with the sun) to bring it to you.

Light the candle and burn it as you gaze at the flame for at least five minutes, concentrating on your goal.

Note: When you are finished candle spell-casting, always snuff the candles, don't blow them out unless the spell says to. Blowing them out blows away their energy.

OTHER STUFF

Ash: From anything burnt binds harmful energies and offers the potential of renewal.

Body bits: Filings from nails, a lock of hair, drops of blood: bind a person's energy to the spell.

Honey: To sweeten and empower.

Ice: Slows or binds an action or energy.

Magnet: Draws and attracts a result or energy.

Soil scooped from the imprint of a footprint: Captures a person's energy to bind it to a spell.

White cord that is exactly your height: Captures and
holds your energy and presence.

CRYSTALS

There are many different types of crystals – a lot of them
have similar properties and sometimes the choices are overwhelming! I talk about them at length in *Witch – a Magickal
Year* so here I have listed a few good ones specifically for
Teen Witches.

Amber: Not really a crystal at all but the fossilised resin
of a tree, amber is great for grounding and focusing your
energies.

Amethyst: Peace of mind and as a talisman for restful sleep
and good dreams. Also amplifies psychic ability – very
handy for a Teen Witch!

Black obsidian: Good as a charm to ward away peer pressure.

Citrine: Mental powers (good to have around whilst
studying).

Clear quartz: Good as an overall energy harmoniser for
boys and can give strength and courage.

Fluorite: Another good one for mental powers, especially
artistic expression.

Moonstone: Great for girls (especially worn around
period time).

Opal: Can help release anger and resentment.

Rose quartz: The ultimate love amplifier.

Tiger's eye: Courage and luck, as well as favourable results
from a testing situation (whether a school exam or drivers'
licence).

White agate crystal: Encourages good communication,
purity and the promise of good things to come.

POWERFUL PRESENCES

The Goddess and God and other magickal beings below are all referred to in this book. There are many more (see *Witch – A Magickal Year* for starters) but I have suggested these as an initial way for you to become familiar with the process of invoking and connecting with the energies of these celestial and mythological beings.

There are also some suggested herbs, fruits and flowers which will help you commune with their essence. You can burn the herbs as incense, the fruits can be eaten and the flowers displayed.

THE LADY AND THE LORD

The Lady is the Goddess in her triple aspect of Maiden, Mother and Crone – reflecting the cycles of life, creativity and destruction. She is all things, all faces of the Goddess, omnipresent and eternal.

The Lord is mostly related to by Witches as the Horned God or God of the Forests and Animals (Pan). He interacts with the Goddess as her Son, Lover and Consort and in the Myth of the Wheel of the Year. Like the Sun, he moves in cycles between his growing, light, overworld aspect (from Yule to Litha) and his dark, underworld presence (from Litha to Yule).

ARTEMIS

Greek Goddess of the waxing Moon (called Diana by the Romans).

Sacred to Artemis: Almond blossoms or leaves from the tree, daisies, wormwood (its other name *artemisia absynthium* is named for her).

Artemis is the Goddess of the Crescent Moon and seen as the Waxing or Maiden face of the three faces of the moon. She hunts with a silver bow and arrow and is also an accomplished musician. She is also virginal and very protective of her chastity, and is fierce and proud.

SELENE

Greek Goddess of the full Moon.

Sacred to Selene: Myrrh, jasmine, vervain.

Selene is the Greek Goddess of the Full moon and presides over the fertility and abundance of the land and sea. She is a great source of inspiration and empowerment representing the lush nurturing power of motherhood.

HECATE

Greek Goddess and Patroness of Witches.

Sacred to Hecate: Almond, garlic, myrrh, willow, patchouli.

Hecate is the Goddess of the Dark and Waning moon and she is depicted as a Crone of great age and wisdom. Her realm is the Underworld and she understands better than anyone the cycles of life and death. She also presides over crossroads and these are a good place to leave offerings to her to gain her favour.

APHRODITE

Greek Goddess of Love and the Sea (called Venus by the Romans).

Sacred to Aphrodite: Apple, parsley, rose.

Aphrodite is popularly depicted as rising out of the sea nestled like a pearl in a beautiful scallop shell. She is the patroness of lovers and is particularly good to invoke for self-love and self-worth spells, as her pure yet passionate presence is perfect to absorb when you are feeling down.

BAST
Egyptian Sun Goddess.
Sacred to Bast: Catnip, dragon's blood powder.
Bast is mostly recognised as the Cat Goddess, or as a cat-headed Goddess carrying her instrument, a sistrum (a sacred rattle), an ankh, or the papyrus wand. In early Egyptian mythology she was seen as a fierce avenger and protector of the Pharoah. In later years she became associated with music, sensuality, fertility, and arts. As such, Bast's role started to change, and her status of protector was extended to women, children and families.

RHIANNON
Welsh Goddess of birds and horses.
Sacred to Rhiannon: Lily of the valley, carnations, honeysuckle and vervain.
Rhiannon is also seen in her light and dark aspect as a Goddess who can travel between the Overworld and the Underworld (life and death). She rides a beautiful white mare (symbolic of faithfulness and endurance) and can talk to birds. There is the legend of the three blackbirds of Rhiannon who sing so sweetly that their song puts the listener into a trance so they can access the worlds between the worlds.

MERLYN
Magickal Master of Arthurian legend and Learning, Knowledge and Magickal Wisdom.
Sacred to Merlyn: Dill, marjoram and valerian, myrrh,

amber and hazel wood.

Merlyn was magician, counsellor and entertainer to King Arthur and is considered a Patron of male Witches. He also embodies the spirit of the Lord of the Forests and Woods.

ARCHANGEL MICHAEL

A Judeo-Christian angelic force that I often call upon to help clear away negativity, blockages and sadness. He carries a huge sword that cuts through any psychic dross and I always feel his presence of exciting and empowering, yet also comforting, like a big brother!

Gobbledy Gook!

Altar: A table or similar surface upon which the working tools of a Witch, representations of the Goddess and God, and articles used in spellcraft are placed. A Witch's altar generally faces the Earth Quarter (due South in the southern hemisphere and north in the northern). Altars may either be permanently set up or prepared only when required. In outdoor rituals, stones, tree stumps, etc., are often used as makeshift altars.

Astral realm/astral plane: Terms popularized by theosophy to describe the lower levels of existence, subtler than the physical plane but resembling it closely, all physical objects being believed to have astral equivalents. While theosophy describes the various levels or planes very specifically, the term 'astral' is typically used less precisely in Wicca (and many other magical traditions) to describe a variety of realms of being made of energies subtler than matter though still apparently retaining form. It is widely believed that changes made on the astral bring about changes in physical reality, this principle being used in many forms of magic (such as astral projection, in which the astral equivalent of the body of the Witch or magician is set free to explore and modify that plane).

Athame: A knife, traditionally double-edged and black-handled, used by a Witch to delineate sacred space, astrally inscribe pentagrams and other symbols, and direct energy in consecrations (in spells, the charging of wine, etc). It also represents the power of Air (or, less typically, Fire) and a Witch's identity as a Priest/ess of the Craft. The usual pronunciation is either 'ath-am-ee' or 'ath-arm-ay' – however, since many Witches first learnt the word from books, virtually every other possible pronunciation is likely to be heard.

Bind: (1) To bind a spell is to complete its casting, releasing it to do its work independently of the weaver of the spell. The spell is bound to its desired result and should henceforth only be thought of in terms of its completion, not the manner in which it will work. Some spells incorporate the actual tying of a knot to bind the spell. (2) To bind an individual magically is to use spellcraft to prevent them from behaving in a certain fashion. Some Witches never use such spells, feeling them to be overly manipulative, while others feel they have a duty to do all they can to prevent, for example, a rapist or child molester from repeating their crimes. A binding is very different from a curse since it only prevents specific behaviour, rather than harming an individual. The caster of the spell can, therefore, safely accept the spell's 'return'.

Book of Shadows: A book of spells, rituals and lore, either assembled by the individual Witch according to his or her own tastes and requirements or deriving from one of several Books of Shadows compiled by Gerald Gardner and associates in the 1940s and 50s. The individually assembled Book of Shadows (BOS) is the more widely used type now and their contents may contain everything from magical diaries, recipes and picture collections to transcriptions from grimoires and other magical texts.

Celtic: Relating to a particular Indo-European race thriving in the pre-Roman era in Britain, France and other regions of Western Europe. The remaining strongholds of Celtic culture include Ireland, Scotland, Wales and Brittany. Wicca is strongly influenced by ancient and contemporary Celtic culture and magical traditions but, contrary to many superficial books and articles on the subject, it isn't a Celtic religion or movement – it is, in fact, one of the most multicultural of all spiritual paths. Some traditions, however, do emphasise the Celtic aspects of the Craft, just as others might the Scandinavian, Italian or Jewish aspects.

Chakra: One of seven centres of spiritual energy positioned along the spine and skull of the human body which, when activated through meditation and visualisation allows the flow of a current of energy, enhancing magical and spiritual workings. An Eastern concept, popularized in the West by Theosophy and related organizations, chakra workings are now commonly used by Wiccans of many traditions.

Chalice: A drinking vessel, generally handle-less and comprising a bowl, stem and base, used in Wicca to represent the element of Water. The principal use of the chalice in Wiccan ritual is to contain wine (or mead, water, juice or whatever is preferred) to be blessed by the Goddess and God, then drunk to take that blessing into the body. Where more than one person is in the Circle the chalice is passed, with a kiss, around those assembled to deepen the bonds between them. A chalice may also be used in spellcraft to hold an item of jewellery, etc, being consecrated.

Charcoal disks: Small, flattened cylinders of compressed charcoal used to heat granulated incense. Best lit by holding them with tweezers over a naked flame. Once alight, a disk should be placed in a well-insulated container (a layer of sand is ideal) and a small amount of incense sprinkled on top of it. They are available at most New Age and occult supply shops.

Church: In a Wiccan context, generally a reference to the many forms of Christian Church or, historically, either the Roman Catholic or a significantly powerful Protestant Church. Though occasionally used disparagingly (generally by those viewing it as an historically oppressive, anti-Pagan force), the Christian Church is afforded by most Witches the same respect they accord all religions. Wiccans in general have no grievance with any religious organization or individuals except those who revile and seek to demonize the Craft or any other equally worthy faith.

Circle: A space delineated and sanctified by a Witch or Witches for the purposes of protection or a ritual. A Wiccan Circle may be visibly represented or simply astrally inscribed. The Circle is actually better visualized as a sphere than a boundary on the ground, and as a field of energy rather than a bubble (through which, presumably, one's head would poke out when near the edge!).

Coven: A small group of three or more Witches who regularly join together for Circles. Though the term is often loosely used to describe any group practising the Craft, the Coven should ideally be united by a strong level of commitment to both Witchcraft and the group itself. Bonds between Coven members should be those of very close friends or even family members, and groups of casual acquaintances getting together for an occasional Sabbat or spellcasting are more properly referred to as Groves or simply Open Circles or working groups. The traditional ideal number of members is thought to be thirteen, although in practice this is more like a maximum number of members. Many of the most durable Covens only comprise three to six members.

Collective unconscious: A term from Jungian psychology descriptive of a deep stratum of shared knowledge and insight available to all members of the human race. This shared wealth of information is generally perceived to be encoded in symbols rather than verbal language. The concept was coined to provide a hypothetical explanation for the way in which distantly located cultures with no apparent means of communicating ideas and mythologies often seemed to generate very similar grammars of symbolism.

Correspondences: In magical theory, the kinship of certain sets of ideas or qualities. A keystone of contemporary magical lore is the concept that a deeply encoded unity may be found in superficially different substances, so that, for example, a particular colour, perfume, herb, element, magical tool, planet, zodiacal constellation and day of the week share an inherent quality. Hence, the colour red might be considered to relate to the planet Mars, and the colour green to Venus; the scent of frankincense relate to Jupiter and myrrh to Saturn; and so on. In ritual, a particular energy can be magnified by concentrating as many different related substances and influences together as possible.

Craft, The: One of the terms used loosely to describe either Wicca (see below) or Witchcraft of all varieties. The term was used to describe Freemasonry long before Witchcraft adopted it, suggesting that it is one of many Masonic phrases adopted by Gerald Gardner in his reformulation of the Craft in the 1940s and 50s.

Deosil: Movement in the direction of the sun, hence clockwise in the northern hemisphere (where the sun rises in the east, veers to the south (ie the direction of the Equator), before setting in the west) and anti-clockwise in the southern hemisphere. In Wiccan ritual, sunwise motion tends to be used to draw power in, and counter-sunwise movement to banish or cast energy out. See also Widdershins.

Druidic: Pertaining to the faith of the early Celtic priest and priestesshood or their modern day counterparts. In Britain, Druidery is the second largest Pagan movement after the Craft with which it shares many beliefs and practices.

Etheric plane: A term popularized through Theosophy to describe the energy field interconnecting the physical and astral planes. The etheric is often referred to as 'life force' (and a host of other names) and is the most commonly perceived portion of the aura.

Familiar: A spirit assistant to a Witch. A familiar may be either an elemental or a formerly human spirit, often taking the form of, or actually inhabiting the body of, an animal. It should be stressed, however, that not all Witches' pets are necessarily familiars. Witches enjoy the company of animals for their own sake as much as any intelligent member of the human race does!

Garland: A wreath of leaves, flowers or a combination of both, either worn as a crown or hung up as a decoration. Witches often use seasonal vegetation in garlands to emphasise the season they are currently celebrating.

Gerald Gardner: An Englishman who, in the late 30's and 40's popularized modern Wicca. He established the Gardnerian tradition of Witchcraft and is an important figure in the Craft. Before he claimed to be a Witch he had been involved in other spiritual paths like Co-Masonary and Rosicrucianism and had traveled extensively in the East learning of indigenous spiritual practices of the people. All these influenced his teachings of Wicca. Read his book, 'Witchcraft Today' written in 1954 to find out more.

Guardian: Generally short for 'Guardian of the Watchtower' – one of many images used to personify the elemental powers of each of the four Quarters (see below). Guardians may also be spirits, elemental or otherwise, called to protect a Witch, other individual or even a location from harm.

Hex/hexing: A word derived from a German word for Witch describing the casting of a spell. Although the word itself has no connotation of either positive or negative spellcasting, in common usage the word is used synonymously with 'curse'.

Intuition: A form of perception or thinking not apparently connected to rational structuring of thought. Witches tend to give this form of mental activity equal (or sometimes even superior) status to logical thought, on the basis that the brain comprises two sides, each with its own mode of coming to conclusions.

Invoke: To call a spirit or deity into oneself or one's Circle.

Libations: In Wicca, an offering to the Goddess and God of wine (or another beverage) blessed within the Circle. In an outdoor ritual, the offering may be poured during the Circle; in indoor Circles, the offering is taken out after the closing of the ritual. Though libation literally means an offering of drink, Wiccans frequently extend the meaning to include the offering of whatever food was shared during the Circle as well.

Magick: An archaic spelling of 'Magic' popularized by Aleister Crowley, largely to differentiate it from stage magic –(the 'pulling a rabbit out of a hat' variety). The term has been repeatedly redefined by modern occultists and Witches but essentially refers to the manipulation of reality by apparently supernatural means by the will of an individual or group.

Metaphysical: In general usage synonymous with supernatural. Some Witches also interpret this is to mean 'pertaining to matters not yet understood by science'.

Occult/occultist: The 'occult' is another term for that which is hidden, ie that which is not yet understood by conventional wisdom. An occultist is, therefore, one who studies those subjects that exist within human experience but outside established understanding.

Ouija board: A board on which alphabetical (and related) characters are marked out and upon which an indicator (traditionally an inverted glass or a planchette – a small board on wheels) is held by the fingertips of two or more people in the hopes that disincarnate spirits will be able to communicate. Popularized by Spiritualism, Ouija boards are rarely used by Witches, who tend to feel that inviting any passing spirit into their bodies or homes is slightly more dangerous than leaving the front door open in a high-crime neighbourhood.

Path: In this book 'Path' refers to the practice of Witchcraft by an individual – emphasizing the 'journey' aspect of their practices

Patriarchy: A social system in which males are dominant.

Pentacle: A disc or stone inscribed with a pentagram and possibly other esoteric symbols representing the element of Earth. The pentacle can be used to hold objects being consecrated, to act as a shield against unwanted energy or to help ground energy. An alternative to the pentacle as a Craft tool symbolising Earth in some Wiccan traditions is a stone (often polished into a spherical shape). The word 'pentacle' is often also casually used to mean a pendant, ring or earring inscribed or molded into the shape of a pentagram.

Pentagram: A regular five-pointed star used as a symbol of blessing and power in many magical traditions, including the Craft. The five points are often said to represent the four elements giving rise to the fifth – the element of spirit. For this reason the pentagram is generally shown with one point uppermost, representing the ascent of spirit through balanced matter, while the inverted pentagram is often seen as a symbol of the spirit in decline (hence its use in negative magic and Satanism). However, in Gardnerian Craft, the inverted pentagram is used as a symbol of their Second Degree and in that context shouldn't be mistaken for a malevolent symbol.

Petitions: as referred to in this book, wishes and requests written on paper and thrown into fire or the air to bring in the power of these elements to make them come true.

Power finger: The index finger of a witch's dominant hand (ie the one they write with or generally favour). The magical tools of a Witch are ultimately just objects used to help fire up the imagination and so can be dispensed with for workings when necessary. In workings where an athame, sword or wand are unavailable or impractical, a finger can be used to direct energy equally efficiently.

Quarter: Within a Witch's Circle, one of the cardinal points of the compass, each of which corresponds to one of the four Elements. Correspondences will vary from tradition to tradition and place to place but the quartered Circle is one of the most common features of Wiccan ritual.

Runes: Alphabetical characters used by Germanic and Scandinavian people up till the Middle Ages. The original runes were associated with a number of magical correspondences and have recently been revived as a tool for divination. A rune may also be a short poem used as a spell or invocation.

Satanism: A form of inverted Christianity where the vices of the Christian faith are held to be virtues and vice versa. Despite some superficial similarity in magical tools and trappings, there is no theological or philosophical connection between Wicca, a form of Pagan religion/spirituality and Satanism.

Sigil: A sign or symbol supposedly possessed of an inherent magical power.

Skyclad: A term borrowed from Jainism (a very disciplined religion of India) by Gerald Gardner to describe nakedness as a state of power and sacredness rather than vulnerability. While some Wiccan traditions work clothed in robes, costumes or even street clothes, the tradition of skyclad working remains popular since it emphasizes several qualities necessary to the Craft: self-acceptance, individuality, freedom and mutual trust.

Solitary: A Witch who practises the Craft alone most of the time, whether by choice or circumstance. Most Witches who are part of Covens or other working groups still work solitary at least some of the time. While the Gardnerian Book of Shadows stated one couldn't be 'a Witch alone', contemporary thinking is of the opinion that a Witch needs to do just that periodically to avoid becoming dependant on group energy.

Taoism: A Chinese religion/philosophy with a number of similarities to the Craft, notably an emphasis on spiritual polarity (in Taoism conceived of as Yin and Yang; in Wicca, as the God and Goddess) and the interconnectedness of all things. Traditional Taoism also has a strong magical element, and recommends alignment with the natural flow of life's energy.

Teutonic: Relating to either the Teuton tribes who lived in Jutland and southern France until falling to Rome, or to Germanic people and culture in general.

Theosophy: From the Greek *theos* (god, divinity) and *sophia* (wisdom), meaning divine wisdom. The Theosophical Society is a religious society founded in the late 1800's by a woman, Helena Petrovna Blavatsky (H P Blavatsky) and two men, H.S. Olcott and W.Q. Judge. They introduced Oriental philosophical and religious ideas to the west, like concepts of reincarnation and karma. A primary idea is the essential oneness of all beings – all things are linked cosmically.

Third eye: One of the chakras, positioned in the centre of the forehead and associated with the pineal gland. The chakra is related to the power of inner vision, both active visualisation and the ability to see 'between' the worlds.

Wand: A length of wood, often decorated with carvings and tipped with crystals, used in Witchcraft to represent the element of Fire (or, less typically, Air). The wand was originally conceived as a symbol of authority in magic and is frequently described as being used in commanding spirits and the like. In the Craft, it is more often used to direct energy either into an object or (in the case of healing energy, for example) out of the Circle and towards a spell's target. Since Fire also relates to the Will, the wand is often held aloft in the making of oaths or the proclaiming of an intention.

Western magick: The magical practices associated with the Western Mystery tradition, an array of systems given the collective name to differentiate them from Indian and Far Eastern esoteric magical practices. Many influential occult organisations such as the Theosophical Society have had eras in which they championed Eastern traditions but showed little interest in ancient European esoteric traditions. While much of value was imported to Europe by these organisations, many occultists felt their own cultures were being dangerously neglected, hence the emphasis on the West.

Wicca: A contemporary form of Pagan Witchcraft owing much to the mid-twentieth century work of Gerald Gardner. While Gardner represented Wicca as being a magical tradition existing for centuries in much the form described in his books, it's now clear that he was much more like the innovative, creative Wiccans of today, formulating his own vision of Witchcraft from a wide range of influences. Wicca wasn't Gardner's invention any more than rock and roll was Elvis Presley's. Both, however, were enormously influential in changing and popularizing their chosen fields. Using the word 'Wicca' in this sense is useful in differentiating modern Pagan Witchcraft from the many other species of Witchery around the world.

Widdershins: Movement in the opposite direction to that of the sun, hence anti-clockwise in the northern hemisphere and clockwise in the southern hemisphere. See also Deosil.

Websites, Suppliers and Suggested Reading

WEBSITES

www.fionahorne.com

Visit my website for regular updates on what I've been getting up to as well as lots of photos, articles, competitions and cool links to other Teen Witch sites, suggested reading and lots more including suppliers. I am proud to say that fionahorne.com, created and maintained by myself, Tracey Shaw and Lauren O'Keefe, is consistently in the Top 10 of most popular Australian websites! Thanks for your support!

SUPPLIERS

NSW

Adyar Bookshop, 230 Clarence St, Sydney NSW 2000
Ph: (02) 9267 8509; www.adyar.com.au

Mysterys
1st floor, 314–322 Darling St, Balmain NSW 2041
Ph: (02) 9818 2274
Lush Cosmetics
For information for your nearest stockist, call (02) 9700 9360, or visit their website at www.lush.com.au

VICTORIA

Esotoric Bookshop, Glen Arcade, 675 Glenferrie Rd, Hawthorn, VIC 3122; Ph: (03) 9818 1998; www.estorericbookshop.com.au

Spellbox – for product and stocklist information call (03) 9525 6445

SOUTH AUSTRALIA

Marbri Witchcraft Shop, 1/581 North East Road, Gilles Plains, SA 5086; Ph: (08) 8266 4082

QUEENSLAND

Wizard's Realm, Shop 25, The Mark Centre, 3-15 Orchid Avenue Surfers Paradise, QLD 4218; Ph: (07) 5538 3445

The Witches Cauldron, Shop 9, 79 Grafton St, Cairns QLD 4870 Ph: (07) 4051 2100; witches@internetnorth.com.au

WESTERN AUSTRALIA

The Alchemist, 6 Market St, Fremantle, WA 6160; Ph: (08) 9430 6779

WITCHCRAFT MAGAZINE

This national magazine just gets better and better – it is now bi-monthly and not only has wonderful regular writers but also special guests like the very well-respected Nevill Drury (author of some favourite occult books of mine, *Pan's Daughter* and *Other Temples, Other Gods*). The magazine also has a very good advertising content that will help if you're looking for contacts and suppliers in your State. Pick it up in most newsagencies or subscribe by calling FPC Magazines Customer Service on (02) 9353 9992.

SUGGESTED READING

It seems like a new book on Witchcraft is published every day! Here are a few brand new titles I'd like to recommend (you may like to check out the extensive 'Library' sections in *Witch – A Personal Journey* and *Witch – A Magickal Year* for a comprehensive introduction to various new and classic titles).

Love Magic (1999)
The Girls' Handbook of Spells (2000)
Both by Antonia Beattie, published by Lansdowne Press
Antonia is a wonderful writer and really knows her Witchy stuff! Love
magic is a saturated subject yet Antonia manages to come up with a
new and inspiring approach to it! And no girl Witch can be without
her brand new collection of sure-fire spells!

The Triumph of the Moon (1999)
by Ronald Hutton, published by Oxford University Press
This one is a pretty in-depth read but it's absolutely the most important book to come out on the *real* history of the Craft since the infamous book *Drawing Down the Moon* by Margot Adler. Grab a copy and
take your time reading it.

Witchcraft Theory and Practice (2000)
by Ly Warren Clarke, published by Llewellyn
This is a reworked *Way of the Goddess* – the classic volume by Ly which
was the first book I ever read about the Craft. I interviewed Ly in
Witch – A Personal Journey and I am thrilled her book is available again.
She is an amazing woman and Witch!

The Witches of Eileanan series
By Kate Forsyth, published by Random House
Dragonclaw (1997); *Pool of Two Moons* (1998); *The Cursed Towers* (1999);
The Forbidden Land (2000)
Coming soon are *The Skull of the World* and *The Fathomless Caves*
Kate is an Australian writer and these books are not only great fantasy
novels but loaded with well researched information on Witchcraft.
They're impossible to put down!

FIONA HORNE'S WIKID WITCH KIT
(available at Myers and Stuf stores)

In creating my WIKID WITCH KIT I hope to take you on a magickal and exciting journey! Through music, song, spoken word and ritual I want to help you unleash your inner magick and discover the wonderful and positively empowering world of Witchcraft.

As a part of this journey you will discover your WIKID magickal name, giving you access to an exclusive website and online coven. There you can meet up with other Wikid Witches to swap spells, stories and ideas.

And every full moon I will join you for a special online gathering – which will be truly WIKID!
The Wikid Witch Kit features:

Wikid Magick Fizz
Take a magickal bath in this scented bath fizz! It works with the elements of earth (salts) and water to purify and ground.

Wikid Magick Potion
Anoint yourself with this shimmery body potion and you're ready to make magick! It works to connect the physical with the spirit (magickal potion application) and is the final preparation for the magickal ritual.

Wikid Magick Fire
Light the five wicks to invoke the sacred elements. Each wick represents the four physical elements – fire, air, earth, water – and the directions they are found in – north, south, east, west as well as Spirit, which is found in the centre.

Wikid Magick Star
Meditate on the star to fuel your inner power. This is a special interpretation of the Witches Pentagram (a five pointed star). This is printed on the cover of the CD as a magickal talisman to encourage focus and contemplation.

Wikid Magick Cord
Seal your powers for future use with this magick cord.

Wikid Magick Journey CD
The journey begins and never ends here!

The Wikid Witch Kit also features a magickal concoction of essential oils blended by me to inspire and empower you!
   Orange: to focus the intellect and promote a sense of tranquillity
   Ylang Ylang: to connect with the spirit, intuition and to enhance feelings of self love
   Sandalwood: purifying, sacred and empowering.

I get a lot of emails and letters from Teen Witches wondering where they can first start to explore their inner magickal talents which is why I have created, the WIKID WITCH KIT. Its contents, and the ritual I have created will get you on the Path of the Craft and give you the opportunity to connect with other Wikid Witches – including me! I look forward to welcoming you to the world of Wikid Witches!

Blessed Be★
FIONA★